Breed Stand...
for the Lhasa ...

SIZE
Ideal height: dogs 25.4 cms (10 ins) at shoulders;
bitches slightly smaller.

NECK
Strong and well arched.

BODY
Length from point of shoulders to point of buttocks
greater than height at withers. Well ribbed. Level
topline. Strong loin. Balanced and compact.

HINDQUARTERS
Well developed with good muscle. Good
angulation. Heavily furnished with
hair. Hocks when viewed from
behind parallel and not too
close together.

TAIL
High-set, carried well over the back but not like
a pot-hook. Often a kink at end. Well
feathered.

COAT
Top coat long, heavy, straight, hard
neither woolly nor silky. Moderate
undercoat.

FEET
Round, cat-like with firm pads.
Well feathered.

COLOUR
Golden, sandy, honey, dark grizzle,
slate, smoke, parti-colour, black,
white or brown. All equally acceptable.

Lhasa Apso

◇

by Juliette Cunliffe

Table of Contents

9

29

DISTRIBUTED BY:

INTERPET
P U B L I S H I N G
Vincent Lane, Dorking, Surrey RH4 3YX England

ISBN 13: 978 1 902389 17 2

98

121

148

The History of the
LHASA APSO

The enchanting little Lhasa Apso, considered by its admirers to be a big dog in a small body, hails from Tibet, the land known as 'The Roof of the World.' This mystical country with its barren landscape lies at a high altitude. Inhabitants, both human and canine, have to be able to deal with extremes of temperature and fiercely bright light. The Tibetans are a stalwart race, and truly typical Apsos carry many traits similar to those of their original owners.

The Lhasa Apso is said to have existed since 800 BC, but there is no tangible evidence of this as written historical records in Tibet were not kept until around AD 639. Buddhism spread from India into Tibet during the seventh century. In this faith the lion, in its various mythological forms, plays an important part. Indeed the Buddha Manjusri, the god of learning, is believed to travel around as a simple priest with a small dog. This dog, although not an Apso, can instantly be transformed into a lion so that the Buddha can ride on its back.

It is the snow lion, though, that is considered the king of animals and it is with this white

Ch Tabbi Tu of Jonters, co-owned by Juliette Cunliffe and Carol Ann Johnson.

mythological beast that the Lhasa Apso is most closely connected. The snow lion is believed to be so powerful that when it roars seven dragons fall out of the sky.

Lhasa Apsos have sometimes been said to be sacred animals, but this is not so. They were certainly kept in monasteries, primarily to give a warning bark to the monks if ever intruders or uninvited guests managed to get

Opposite page: The author and one of her Apsos enjoying the snow.

9

Tibetan Spaniels with their pet cat.

past the enormous Tibetan Mastiffs tethered outside. Nonetheless, the breed was held in high esteem. The dogs historically never were sold, but given only as gifts, for Lhasa Apsos are believed to carry the souls of monks who erred in their previous lives. Such dogs were also given as tribute gifts for safe passage from Tibet to China, a long journey by caravan that took eight to ten months.

Although Tibetans have always drawn distinction between the 'true' lion and the 'dog' lion, they have never been too clear about the naming of their breeds. Without doubt some crossing took place between the various Tibetan breeds. Even today it is possible to breed together two fully-coated Lhasa Apsos and to produce one or more puppies that look like purebred Tibetan Spaniels. This may come

as something of a shock, but is clearly a throwback to earlier days. Interestingly, the Tibetans refer to all long-coated dogs as 'Apsok,' which further complicates the issue when trying to research the history of Tibetan breeds.

THE LHASA APSO'S RELATIONSHIP WITH OTHER BREEDS

The term 'Apsok,' or 'Apso,' is also used to describe the Tibetan Terrier, a longer-legged cousin of the Lhasa Apso. We are the ones, in the West, who have had the temerity to add the word 'Lhasa' to the breed's name, although clearly it was necessary to draw some distinction between the various Tibetan breeds. When these breeds first arrived in Britain there was great confusion amongst them.

DID YOU KNOW?

The breed has been known as 'Apso Seng Kyi,' said to have been translated as 'Bark Sentinel Lion Dog.' However, the author considers a more accurate translation is actually 'hairy moustached lion dog.' Another possible translation, depending upon interpretation, could be 'barking hairy lion dog.'

A Tibetan Mastiff. These large dogs, along with Lhasa Apsos, were often kept in monasteries to protect from intruders.

Tibetan Terriers, mother and daughter.

In the distant past it appears that the Lhasa Apso descended from European and Asiatic herding dogs, including the Hungarian Puli and Pumi. Certainly the breed has very close connections with two of the Tibetan breeds, the Tibetan Terrier and Tibetan Spaniel, a close relation of which is the little-known Damchi of neighbouring Bhutan. Another breed closely related to the Apso is the Shih Tzu; because of the similar outward appearance, the two breeds are frequently confused even today. However, the Shih Tzu was actually developed in China, although its roots go back to the Lhasa Apso of Tibet.

Opposite page: The Tibetan Terrier, shown here, bears quite a resemblance to its cousin, the Lhasa Apso.

THE BREED'S INTRODUCTION TO THE WEST

It has been erroneously quoted all too often that the Lhasa Apso first came to Britain in 1928, but it is essential to realise that the breed was here long before then. The first Lhasa Apso reported in Britain was in 1854, and certainly there were several representatives of the breed in Britain leading up the turn of the twentieth century. There was, though, great confusion surrounding the naming of breeds at this time, and Lhasa Apsos and Tibetan Terriers founds themselves variously referred to as Thibetan, Kashmir, Bhuteer or Lhassa Terriers, and even as Thibet Poodles. In tracing back breed records, I have found different puppies from individual litters registered under a number of different breed names, which exacerbates the problem to no end.

DID YOU KNOW?

Sherpa Tenzing Norgay, who climbed Mount Everest with Sir Edmund Hillary, owned Lhasa Apsos. He was given two by a Tibetan monk and took both with him to his home in Darjeeling, where he founded a kennel. Tenzing took a keen interest in the breed and enjoyed watching the breed on his visits to the UK.

Shih Tzu, shown here, look very similar to Lhasa Apsos; the two breeds are often mistaken for each other.

DID YOU KNOW?

In 1933 it was reported that the Lhasa Apso Prince Haja of Tibet was actually bought as a mongrel for the sum of 15 shillings. He had been purchased from a monkey cage in Bedford. His owners had never heard of the breed but, having discovered what he was, registered the dog under his new name with The Kennel Club as 'Pedigree and breeder unknown.'

Because there were both Lhasa Apsos and Tibetan Terriers in Britain at that time, some were described as being as small as Maltese Terriers, but others as large as Russian Poodles. Clearly the discrepancies arose because there was, indeed, more than one breed. Something that all the dogs had in common was that their tails curled over their backs, a highly Tibetan characteristic of several different breeds known today.

PRE-WORLD WAR I

There are some enchanting stories revolving around some of the earliest Apsos to leave Tibet. We hear of one that was carried on the saddle for miles and miles, with an attendant wreathed in turquoise. However, Apsos did not only belong to the very wealthy—one called Tuko was purchased from a market cart, the contents of which he was quite prepared to defend until grim death!

The Hon Mrs McLaren Morrison imported several foreign breeds to Britain. One of several Lhasa Apsos she owned was Bhutan, renowned for begging at dog shows to raise money for the war fund. Even Princess Alexandra, a regular and enthusiastic visitor to shows, was known to have remarked that the little dog looked as if he

The rare Pumi seems to be closely associated with the early development of the Lhasa Apso.

was begging to leave the show. Sadly Bhutan contracted distemper and, said his owner, '…died at his post, so to speak.' Apparently he kept his end up until the very last, but kept sinking into a sitting position and finally went home to die.

INITIAL CHAMPIONSHIP STATUS

The breed known today as the Lhasa Apso gained championship status in Britain in 1908, although at this time it was shown in different classes for two different sizes, thus accommodating the Tibetan Terrier as well. One of the earliest champions of the breed, Ch Rupso, was imported from Shigatse in 1907. When he died,

his body was stuffed and preserved in the British Museum at Tring. To this day Rupso is still labelled in the museum as a 'Tibetan Terrier,' although he was definitely a Lhasa Apso and measures 25 cms (slightly under 10 ins) in height at withers.

BETWEEN THE FIRST AND SECOND WORLD WARS

The war years took their toll on the breed and the Lhasa Apso was amongst several breeds that struggled to survive. In 1921 Colonel Bailey took over from Sir Charles Bell as Political Officer for Tibet, and Colonel Bailey and his wife brought back Apsos to Britain in 1928. This was the beginning of a traumatic time to

The elegant beauty of a champion-quality Lhasa Apso. Apsos can be appreciated in almost all colours, as the standard does not favour one colour over another.

The Hungarian Puli is often thought of as being an early ancestor of the Apso. The Hungarian language derives from Mongolian, so perhaps there is proof of an ancient connection.

Opposite page: Lhasa Apsos are now popular in countries around the world. The breed standards might vary slightly from country to country, but the dogs themselves look very much alike.

follow, for soon after Shih Tzu were also imported to Britain from China and initially some thought them to be the same breed as the Lhasa Apso.

At first these dogs were shown together in the same classes, but differences were noted. The difference in length of forefaces was especially noted, leading to what was to become known as 'the war of the noses.' The ladies and gentlemen of the day who enthused about the breeds from Tibet and China engaged in heated, but polite, debate. The

Kennel Club also became involved. Finally the differences were resolved and in 1934 breed standards were laid down for the Lhasa Apso, Tibetan Terrier, Tibetan Spaniel and Tibetan Mastiff. The Shih Tzu was classified as a separate breed and was not represented by the newly formed Tibetan Breeds Association.

The breed had now finally arrived on a firm footing, but it did not compare with the popularity of the breed today. In 1935 only 12 Lhasa Apsos were

A lovely Apso puppy is Modhish Mumbo Jumbo Millie at about one month of age. Her striking colour pattern is evident even at a very young age.

Opposite page: The Shih Tzu, shown here, is often confused with the Lhasa Apso. Both breeds, when kept in full coat, need considerable grooming to look this beautiful.

DID YOU KNOW?

When the division of the breeds was underway in the early 1930s, rather heated meetings were held at the home of Lady Freda Valentine in London's Green Street. In her inimitable way, Lady Freda used to ask one of the most difficult ladies present if she would pass around the cream cakes. This caused her to be obliged to speak to others attending the meeting, and they to her, thus breaking the ice.

entered at Crufts, which gives an indication of how little the breed was known in Britain at that time.

THE LHASA APSO GOES TO THE USA

An American by the name of Suydam Cutting had sent four dogs to His Holiness the Dalai Lama by way of a gift. As a result, a correspondence friendship developed between them and in 1933 HH the Dalai Lama sent two Lhasa Apsos to Mr Cutting and his wife. Two more Apsos followed and then, in 1950, HH the 14th Dalai Lama sent another pair. The latter pair, Le and Phema, both became American champions. Although other people also played an important part in the Lhasa Apso's early history in the USA, it was largely through the Cuttings and their Hamilton Kennels that the breed initially found its place in the American show scene.

The American breed standard was drawn up in 1935 but during the breed's early years in America, confusion raised its head once again. Between the years of 1937 and 1950 some dogs had been imported to the USA, where they had been registered in good faith as Lhasa Apsos. Unfortunately, they were actually Shih Tzu. Between these years, and before their true identity was recognised, some of the dogs were bred from. In consequence many American Lhasa

Apsos carry Shih Tzu blood in their pedigrees, although this does not apply to all as some lines remained clear in those formative years.

EFFECTS OF THE SECOND WORLD WAR IN BRITAIN

There was severe curtailment of breeding programmes during the Second World War, and in Britain many people had their dogs destroyed. Thankfully, it was recognised that for lesser known breeds such drastic measures would spell disaster. Therefore, breeders of Lhasa Apsos were amongst others who were urged to make every effort to help their breeds survive through those difficult times, provided that their dogs were not eating food that would deprive humans.

Between 1939 and 1944 only ten new puppies were registered in the breed, and late in the 1940s Miss Marjorie Wild's important Cotsvale strain was wiped out by hardpad and distemper. Thankfully the breed did manage to survive through some Ladkok- and Lamleh-bred dogs, these descending from the Baileys' imports from Tibet. It was clear, though, that bloodlines had dwindled and had once again to be built up. Just a handful of Lhasa Apsos, largely of unknown pedigree, was imported from Tibet before the Chinese banned all movement of dogs from the country.

Opposite page: There was such a size difference among the first Lhasa Apsos in Britain that some of them were comparable in size to the Maltese, shown here, even though the breeds are not related.

Difficult times during the Second World War forced Lhasa Apso breeders to spare no effort in ensuring the survival of their breed.

Apsos at home in the Himalayas. These dogs look much different than those in full show coat.

THE 1950s

Numbers of Kennel Club registrations had risen gradually so that by 1956 it was felt that the breed was strong enough to break away from the Tibetan Breeds Association and form its own club. This saw the beginning of the Lhasa Apso Club, even though there were only 27 members at the club's first Annual General Meeting and fewer than half of them owned Apsos.

In 1959 the name of the breed was changed to Tibetan Apso, as it felt that this was the only breed from Tibet that did not bear the country's name. However, the change of name did not last long; by 1970 the name had once again reverted to Lhasa Apso.

CHAMPIONSHIP STATUS REGAINED

It was in May of 1964 that the English Kennel Club announced that Lhasa Apso registrations were sufficient in number for Challenge Certificate status to be restored. The first set of Challenge Certificates (CCs) went on offer in 1965, a year in which nine sets were awarded. The first Apso to gain a post-war championship title, by dint of winning three CCs under different judges, was Brackenbury Gunga Din of Verles. Owned by Mrs Daphne Hesketh

Williams, Gunga Din won his third and crowning CC at the West of England Ladies Kennel Society (WELKS) under judge Miss Wild (Cotsvale), who had owned Lhasa Apsos since around the turn of the century.

The winner of the Bitch CC at that same show was Beryl Harding's Brackenbury Chigi-Gyemo, who was the first bitch in the breed to gain her crown, an accolade that came later that same year.

Since then the breed has gone on from strength to strength in Britain, and is one of the most popular breeds in the Utility Group, ranking in the top 20 most popular breeds of all in terms of Kennel Club registrations.

The breed has certainly hit high spots with Ch Saxonsprings Hackensack winning Best in Show at Crufts in 1984, and Ch Saxonsprings Fresno and Ch Saxonsprings Tradition winning Top Dog All Breeds in 1982 and in 1998, respectively.

THE LHASA APSO THROUGHOUT THE WORLD

The Lhasa Apso has made a significant impact on the dog-showing world in many countries, with many enthusiastic support-ers in almost every corner of the globe. The author has been fortunate enough to judge the breed as far south as Australia and as far north as Scandinavia,

finding high-quality specimens in both locations.

In countries where the Lhasa Apso is perhaps not so numerical-ly strong, breeders' enthusiasm seems just as vibrant, for such a remarkable and endearing breed is sure to have admirers wherever it

In Tibet, all long-coated dogs are called 'apsos.'

25

Lhasa Apsos are found worldwide in the homes of discerning dog lovers. It is easy to see why they are appreciated since they are beautiful, intelligent, loyal and obedient.

Apsos are to be found worldwide, even in Iceland and Cuba. While they need a heavy coat for the cold climate of Iceland, the opposite is true for tropical Cuba.

is found. There is now even one solitary Lhasa Apso in Iceland, where this lucky young lady feels very much at home in the snowy clime.

AT HOME IN THE HIMALAYAS

Lhasa Apsos do, of course, still exist in their homeland and in the surrounding Himalayan regions, where they are still very much cherished. One can only hope that the breed in the Western world does not become so excessively glamorised that the Tibetans no longer recognise the stalwart little dog that has shared their lives for so very many generations.

Lhasa Apsos are very family-oriented dogs. They want to live with and become part of their human families. This Apso is quite at home on his own comfortable blanket.

27

LHASA APSO

The Lhasa Apso is undoubtedly an entrancing and enchanting little breed, but its temperament, if typical, is not always easy to understand. In consequence, the Lhasa Apso is not an ideal pet for every home. Although of manageable size, to keep a Lhasa Apso in gloriously long, well-groomed coat takes a lot of work, so that, too, is an important consideration. Some owners of pet Apsos prefer to keep their dogs in short coat; this is perfectly acceptable, but is not suitable for the show ring. Of course regular coat maintenance is still important, whether the coat is kept long or short.

During the last couple of decades the Lhasa Apso has become highly popular, now with well over 3,000 new Kennel Club registrations each year. A Lhasa Apso's winning the accolade of Best in Show at Crufts in 1984 undoubtedly played its part in bringing breed attention to the fore. However, there is much more to an Apso than an elegant dog in full show coat, gliding around a big ring under the spotlights of a major championship show. A Lhasa Apso is a very special dog and needs a very special sort of owner, one who can understand a dog whose ancestors were raised

in a tough environment on 'The Roof of the World.'

PHYSICAL CHARACTERISTICS

The Lhasa Apso is a fairly small breed, though not as small as some. It is sturdy for its size, with good muscle. In Britain the ideal height is 25.4 cms (10 ins) and in theory bitches should be a little smaller. Having said that, size has crept up over the years and in the USA the requirement is for a very slightly taller dog. No weight is specified in the breed standard, but typically a correctly sized Apso is usually between 7 and 8.5 kgs (15.4 and 18.7 lbs), although some are a little heavier.

Even with the hair completely covering the face, the Lhasa Apso's long eyelashes serve to keep the hair out of the dog's eyes.

Opposite page: In the show ring the Lhasa Apso's hair is always worn over the face, but at home most owners tie up the hair in two equal bands.

The head of the breed is often much admired, but the heavy head furnishings somewhat conceal the lovely Tibetan expression. In the show ring the hair is always worn down, but at home the majority of owners tie up the hair in two bands, one on either side of the head. This helps to keep the face hair reasonably clean, avoids breakage of hair at its ends and makes it easier for the dog to see. It is not always realised, though, that the eyelashes of a Lhasa Apso are very long, so the hair does not actually fall into the eye. Obviously in the breed's homeland the hair was never tied up; instead, the head-fall acted as protection against the strong sunlight and whiteness of the snowy terrain.

Because so many people confuse the Lhasa Apso with the Shih Tzu, it is necessary to explain that the head shape of the two breeds is quite different. The skull of the Apso is much narrower than that of the Shih Tzu and the Apso's eye is less round, thus not as prominent. The nose, too, is shorter than that of the Apso, which measures about 4 cms (1.5 ins). There are also differences in body. The rib cage of the Shih Tzu is more barrelled than that of the Apso, and the Shih Tzu is somewhat lower slung.

Unfortunately, the beauty of the Lhasa Apso's coat is sometimes taken to extremes and many owners, out of fear that the

Coat condition is essential to success in the show ring. Some owners do not even let their Apsos outside, except for outdoor shows, for fear of the dogs' soiling or damaging their coats.

Lhasa Apso has not only a long flowing top coat but also a good undercoat. This means that merely grooming the top layer may initially give a reasonably good overall appearance, but in no time at all the undercoat will start to form knots. Knots and tangles are incredibly difficult to remove if allowed to build up, so this aspect of coat care must be taken seriously into consideration before setting one's heart on the breed.

Many Lhasa Apso pets are, however, kept in short coat, known usually as 'pet trim.' Although this can be done at home, many owners find it easier to have the coat professionally trimmed about three times each

dogs will damage their coats, do not allow their dogs the free exercise needed to build up muscle naturally. Provided that an Apso's coat is of typically hard texture and that the coat is cared for regularly, a coat can still retain its glory even when the dog is allowed to exercise freely. Some owners of show Apsos do not allow their dogs to do much more than to spend virtually their whole lives inside crates. These owners may indeed end up with dogs whose coats look good in the show ring, but they do not end up with happy, healthy dogs!

COLOURS AND COAT

A Lhasa Apso in full show coat is a magnificent sight, but to keep a coat in this condition certainly involves time and dedication. The

Lhasa Apsos can be kept in a short coat or a long coat, but only Apsos with full coats can be shown in confor-

DID YOU KNOW?

The Lhasa Apso's homeland, Tibet, is a high table land; the plains around Lhasa are about 3.2 kms (2 miles) above sea level. In size Tibet is equal to France, Germany and Great Britain combined, and temperatures vary considerably. Within the space of a day, temperature may rise from below zero to 38 degrees Centigrade.

Lhasa Apsos occur in many colours. The honey-coloured dog, shown here, is a prime example of a show-quality Lhasa Apso.

A magnificently coloured Apso. This type of colouration is referred to as parti-colour.

Although liver and chocolate coloured Lhasa Apsos are produced from time to time, these are not allowed in the show ring. This is because their nose pigmentation is of corresponding colour to the coat, and the standard states that the nose is to be black.

Because there is no colour preference in Lhasa Apsos, in truth an owner should not be swayed by colour. Having said that, it is only natural that some people have a purely personal preference, just as they might for the colour of their own clothing or household furniture. What really matters are the dog's construction, temperament, general health and coat quality. However, if choosing a pet, colour may indeed be a deciding factor, and this is entirely understandable. After all, there is no point in buying a grey Lhasa Apso and, love the dog as one might, thinking for the next

year. Attention to the coat is, of course, also necessary between trims.

The Lhasa Apso can be found in a wide variety of colours—the breed standard lists golden, sandy, honey, dark grizzle, smoke, parti-colour, black, white and brown. In fact, the list could even be longer, for there are many unusual colour combinations that crop up. A parti-coloured dog is one in which the coat is made up of two distinct colours, one of which is white. Thus one finds gold-and-white, black-and-white, grey-and-white or sable-and-white parti-colours, all of which are equally acceptable.

The mystical look of a well-groomed Lhasa Apso. It is evident why these dogs were often compared to lions in Tibetan mythology.
Inset: Yes, there are eyes hiding under all that hair!

A young Apso puppy being trained to stand on a table. Note the pup's confident look and the majestic curvature of the tail.

fourteen years or so that it was a pity you didn't have the golden colour you really preferred!

TAILS

The tail of the Lhasa Apso should be high set and carried well over the back. Occasionally, if you feel carefully, you may find a small kink at the end of the tail. This is perfectly normal, and you must certainly never endeavour to straighten it out as this would cause injury. This is an old characteristic of the breed that, sadly, now seems to be dying out.

As with the rest of the dog, the tail coat will need regular attention—it, too, is long and flowing. However, because of the breed's size, the Apso's tail is unlikely to knock your precious ornaments onto the floor, as might the enthusiastic tail of a larger dog such as a Dalmatian or Labrador Retriever. The tail of a Lhasa Apso is never docked.

PERSONALITY

The breed standard describes the Lhasa Apso as being alert and steady, but somewhat aloof with strangers. The previous wording of the breed standard incorporated the word 'chary' instead of 'aloof',' and indeed the Australian Kennel Club has reverted to the former standard at the request of breeders.

Whichever of these two words is used, a typical Lhasa Apso will not be overly friendly with strangers, but prefers to take a more reserved stance. An Apso will usually bark as someone approaches the house, then, when the visitor has been welcomed and accepted by the owner, the dog will take a seat at a little distance. From his chosen vantage point the dog will always be able to view what is going on around him, but will only become involved in activities if he so chooses.

Often it takes an Apso some time to make friends, but once he has decided to do so the friendship he offers is sincere. It is always best to allow an Apso to approach any visitor to the home in his own good time; this makes for a much happier eventual relationship.

With family and owners an Apso is very devoted, but not all enjoy a cuddle as much as some owners would like. I have owned many Apsos over the years and have found their personalities each to be individual. Some certainly like more affection than others, and this applies both to

dogs and to bitches.

Apsos can be trained to obedience, but they do have a rather stubborn streak and do not always respond to one's commands as rapidly as one might hope. There is no doubt in my own mind that Apsos like to think things out and that when they do something it has to be because they want to—at least they have to give you that impression!

The Lhasa Apso does give a warning bark, for you will recall

The Lhasa Apso is an alert, steady dog that takes some time to warm up to strangers.

DID YOU KNOW?

Although there is no stipulation as to whether or not dew claws should be removed on the Lhasa Apso, many breeders do like to have them removed when puppies are three days old. This makes nails easier to manage under the long adult coat.

35

Apsos need friends, human and animal! Once a Lhasa Apso decides he likes you, you have a friend for life.

that this is what was expected of the breed in the monasteries of Tibet. However, it is not a particularly high-pitched, piercing bark, and an Apso will usually stop barking quite quickly when he believes the situation is under control.

Although many Apsos get on well with other dogs, there are those that don't. This can depend very largely on upbringing and environment, and sex often has a large part to play in who gets on with whom. Undoubtedly there are some breeders who seem to have absolutely no problem in keeping several males and several females together in one group. However, in my own experience there have been

limitations, and I know that my experiences are shared by many.

Usually bitches will get on well with other females, but they tend to have disagreements around the times of their seasons. Usually this is easily controlled by sensible management but some bitches can have very nasty disagreements, so one should always be on the lookout for

DID YOU KNOW?

The 'puffs' is not a major problem, but it can be alarming and should always be investigated by the owner. There can be other reasons for such puffing; for example, a grass seed could be lodged in the dog's nasal cavity and would require immediate removal.

HEALTH CONSIDERATIONS

Although not usually a serious problem, something that can frighten a new owner is 'the puffs.' This is a fairly frequent occurrence in the brachycephalic (short-nosed) breeds. Because of elongation of the soft palate, a dog will suddenly draw in short, sharp breaths and look very tense, usually standing four square as he does so. This is usually brought on by the dog's becoming very excited, but generally only lasts a matter of seconds. A quick and simple solution is to place one's

A Lhasa Apso truly enjoys being in the company of friends. The young owner seems fairly happy herself!

trouble that may be brewing. Personally, although I have often tried to keep two male Apsos together, I have never succeeded beyond puppyhood, for always argument has ensued. Having said that, I have happily kept one male Apso (not used at stud) with two male Afghan Hounds and the three remained firm friends throughout their lives.

Dogs and bitches usually live together as great friends, but in my own experience I have only successfully kept one male with any number of bitches. Interestingly, I have found that bitches that do not get on together particularly well in their youth seem to mellow with maturity and lose any animosity they may have felt as youngsters.

DID YOU KNOW?

Some Lhasa Apsos are great climbers—some can even scale two-metre-high fences (about 6 feet). Thankfully most do not climb at all, but, since some are

particularly adept, owners must always be aware of this possibility. Much to the surprise of their owners, some do not decide they will take to climbing until they are well into maturity!

37

Lhasa Apsos are hardy dogs but they do, occasionally, inherit an eye condition known as progressive retinal atrophy. This condition slowly leads to total blindness.

fingers over the dog's nostrils, thereby causing him to breathe only through his mouth.

The Lhasa Apso is, in general, a hardy little dog and usually a fairly healthy breed, although there are a few veterinary and possibly hereditary problems that a new owner should be aware of. The only inherited problem officially recognised in the breed is progressive retinal atrophy (PRA). This is an eye disorder, not usually discovered until adulthood, in which a dog progressively goes blind. Often this is noticed first by night blindness, but total blindness is unfortunately the inevitable end result. Thankfully, there is no pain associated with this condition.

PRA has been discovered only recently in the Lhasa Apso and DNA testing is a goal toward which the breed is working, though this may still be a long way off. Currently, it is essential that both the sire and dam of a litter have their eyes tested prior to mating, and breeders have to use carefully their knowledge of hereditary factors to avoid, if possible, doubling up on the gene that carries this inherited disease.

Some Lhasa Apsos seem to suffer from 'dry eye,' something that seems to occur late in life. This can usually be managed with a combination of drugs designed to create artificial tears.

Some Lhasa Apsos are also found to have enlarged harderian glands; this condition is, more specifically, an enlargement of the nictitating membrane in the inner corner of the eye. This is commonly known as 'cherry eye' and is easily noticed as a red swelling. This usually occurs during puppyhood, sometimes in pups as young as about eight weeks of age. There are two methods of dealing with this problem. Currently 'tucking' is the method most commonly used, but it used to be normal just to remove the gland so that the problem could not recur. However, it now appears that when the gland has been removed, the occurrence of 'dry eye' later in life becomes more likely.

Because the Lhasa Apso is a breed that is relatively long-backed and low to the ground, one should always be on the alert for possible back problems, especially in a dog's later years. In an ideal world, Apsos should not be allowed to jump off furniture, but this is more easily said than done! At any sign of spinal injury, a vet should be contacted without delay; in some cases even complete recovery can be achieved. Unfortunately often partial paralysis results, but an affected dog can be fitted with a little wheeled trolley to support his hind legs if the owner so desires. Obviously, caring for a dog who has suffered spinal injuries involves making serious decisions and all of the options, however distressful, must be discussed openly with one's family and vet.

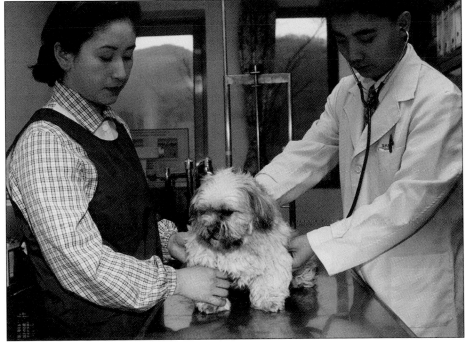

Cleaning the area around the Lhasa Apso's eyes and checking to make sure the eyes look healthy should be part of the everyday grooming routine.

In Korea, where the breed is very much appreciated, a veterinary surgeon at the Samsung Toy Dog Kennel examines a Lhasa Apso.

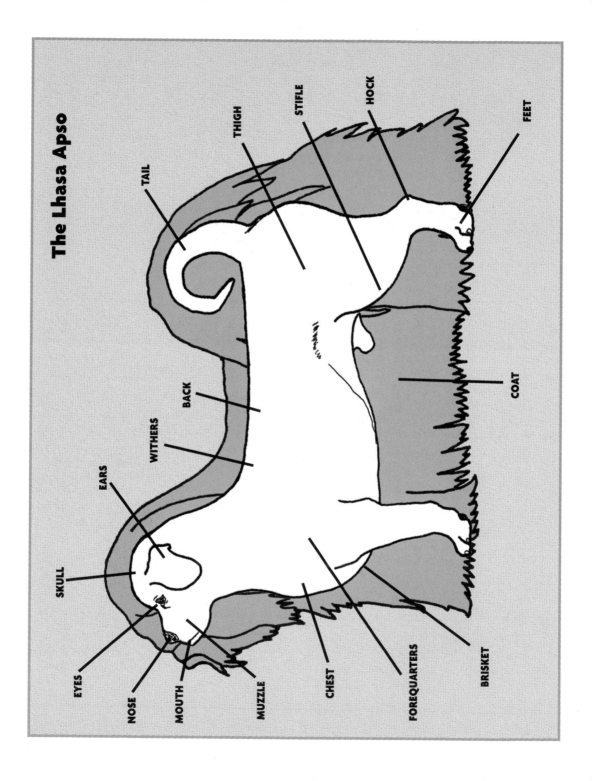

The Lhasa Apso

SKULL

EARS

WITHERS

BACK

TAIL

THIGH

STIFLE

HOCK

FEET

COAT

EYES

NOSE

MOUTH

MUZZLE

CHEST

FOREQUARTERS

BRISKET

Breed Standard for the
LHASA APSO

The Kennel Club breed standard for the Lhasa Apso is effectively a 'blueprint' for the breed. It sets down the various points of the dog in words, enabling a visual picture to be conjured up in the mind of the reader. However, this is more easily said than done. Not

Champion-quality dogs and bitches are used for breeding in order to perpetuate the best qualities of the Lhasa Apso.

only do standards vary from country to country, but people's interpretations of breed standards vary also. It is this difference of interpretation that makes judges select different dogs for top honours, for their opinions differ as to which dog most closely fits the breed standard. That is not to say that a good dog does not win regularly under different judges, or that an inferior dog may rarely even be placed at a show, at least not amongst quality competition.

The breed standard given here is that authorised by the English Kennel Club, but in the American Kennel Club's breed standard size is more flexible, reading, 'Variable, but about 10 inches or 11 inches at shoulder for dogs, bitches slightly smaller.' Another significant difference is in the section on mouth and muzzle, for in America the standard states that the preferred bite is 'level or slightly undershot.' Readers of the following English standard will notice that in Britain, and in consequence in many other countries, a reverse scissor bite is required. In fact, the standard several years ago did include the level bite, but this has since been changed.

In more recent years, two other significant changes were made to the breed standard in Britain. First, the description of 'dense undercoat' was altered to 'moderate undercoat.' Second,

English and Australian Ch. Nedlik Domino at Botolph, co-owned/bred by Jim Bainbridge and Robert Bradley in the U.K., and co-owned by Peter Warby in Australia.

the important phrase 'black ear tips an asset' was written out of the standard, much to the dismay of the author, who was vehemently opposed to this change in particular.

It is true that for the show ring, most of the undercoat is groomed out for purposes of presentation. However, we must never lose sight of the fact that the Lhasa Apso comes from a land with extremes of climate where a good undercoat is imperative for survival.

Moving on to the thorny question of the black ear tips, although perhaps not evident to non-breeders, this is related to the black nose pigment required in the standard. Breeding together, over a prolonged period of time, Apsos that carry no black coat pigment at all eventually causes a loss of depth of skin pigment. This can be seen especially on the nose, which loses colour not only in the winter months when 'winter nose' can all too often be used as an excuse for poor pigmentation.

THE KENNEL CLUB STANDARD FOR THE LHASA APSO
General Appearance: Well balanced, sturdy, heavily coated.

Characteristics: Gay and assertive.

Temperament: Alert, steady but somewhat aloof with strangers.

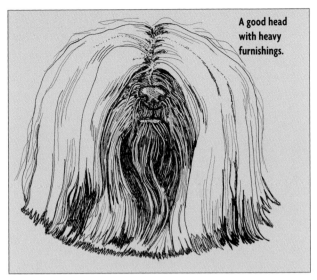

A good head with heavy furnishings.

Incorrect domed head.

Head and Skull: Heavy head furnishings with good fall over eyes, good whiskers and beard. Skull moderately narrow, falling away behind eyes, not quite flat, but not domed or apple headed.

43

Muzzle length should be about one third of the distance from tip of nose to back of skull.

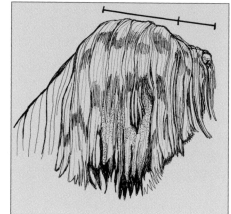

Balanced body with level topline.

Straight foreface with medium stop. Nose black. Muzzle about 4 cms (1.5 ins), but not square; length from tip of nose roughly one third of total length from nose to back of skull.

Incorrect topline; sway back.

Eyes: Dark. Medium size, frontally placed, oval, neither large nor full, nor small and sunk. No white showing at base or top.

Ears: Pendant, heavily feathered.

Mouth: Upper incisors close just inside lower, i.e., reverse scissor bite. Incisors in a broad and as

straight a line as possible. Full dentition desirable.

Neck: Strong and well arched.

Forequarters: Shoulders well laid back. Forelegs straight, heavily furnished with hair.

(left) Correct eyes that are dark, medium in size and oval. (middle) Incorrect eyes that are too large and round. (right) Incorrect; whites of eyes are visible at the base.

Body: Length from point of shoulders to point of buttocks greater than height at withers. Well ribbed. Level topline. Strong loin. Balanced and compact.

Hindquarters: Well developed with good muscle. Good angulation. Heavily furnished with hair. Hocks when viewed from behind parallel and not too close together.

Feet: Round, cat-like with firm pads. Well feathered.

Tail: High-set, carried well over back but not like a pot-hook. Often a kink at end. Well feathered.

Gait/Movement: Free and jaunty.

Coat: Top coat long, heavy, straight, hard neither woolly nor silky. Moderate undercoat.

Colour: Golden, sandy, honey, dark grizzle, slate, smoke, parti-colour, black, white or brown. All equally acceptable.

Size: Ideal height: dogs: 25.4 cms (10 ins) at shoulders; bitches slightly smaller.

Faults: Any departure from the foregoing points should be considered a fault and the seriousness with which the fault should be regarded should be in exact proportion to its degree.

Correct high-set tail, carried over back.

Note: Male animals should have two apparently normal testicles fully descended into the scrotum.

The Lhasa Apso's breed standard is fairly self explanatory, but readers interested in showing their Apso should learn as much as possible from established breeders and exhibitors. It is sensible to attend specialist breed seminars, often hosted by breed clubs. Here the finer points of the breed can be explained fully and discussed. There are, however, a

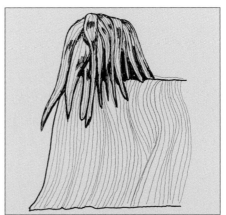

Incorrect 'pot-hook' tail.

few points that benefit from further elaboration.

Those not familiar with the Lhasa Apso often find it difficult to understand the construction of the mouth and placement of teeth. Often a new pet owner can be thoroughly dismayed when, upon taking his new puppy along to the vet for the first time, he is wrongly told that the pup's mouth is incorrect. The mouth should have a reverse scissor bite, meaning that the upper teeth close just inside the lower. This is a highly functional bite, but the teeth should not be set into the jaw such that they protrude at a severe angle. This not only looks untypical but is not at all a practical set of teeth. On the other hand, a slightly undershot mouth with firm teeth correctly set into the jaw is also a functional bite, although not desirable in this breed. Level bites, in which the incisors meet edge to edge, are still occasionally found in the breed, as are scissor bites. Another anomaly is the 'parrot mouth,' which is severely overshot. Thankfully, this is a rare occurrence. 'Parrot mouth' is highly undesirable, so any puppies born with such a mouth should never be bred from.

It should be noted that full dentition is desirable, and although in Britain judges do not count pre-molar and molar teeth in this breed, there should be six upper and six lower incisors set between the canine teeth.

A point that is not mentioned in the standard is the chin. However, all dedicated Apso breeders will agree that an Apso does need to have some chin to give the desired 'Oriental' expression. Most dogs with correct reverse scissor bites or less-correct undershot bites do have sufficient chin, although there are exceptions.

Looking at the head of the Lhasa Apso in profile, the proportion from tip of nose to stop versus stop to back of skull should be 1 to 2. Thus, this is actually a partially brachycephalic breed (partially short-nosed).

Length is measured from 'point of shoulders to point of

Best in Show! This Lhasa Apso takes the top prize at a breed show in Australia.

buttocks.' This is the foremost point of the shoulder blade, not the top tip of the blade as has sometimes been misreported. Thus, in effect, the Apso is really not much longer than the majority of breeds of dog. It should certainly not be so long that it resembles a train!

Movement of the Lhasa Apso has but two words to describe it in the breed standard, 'Free and jaunty.' An incorrect action found in the hind movement of many Apsos today is that the full pads of the hind feet show as the dog moves away. This is the correct movement for a Shih Tzu, but certainly not for a Lhasa Apso. When an Apso moves away, one should only be able to see a third of the pad, for the feet should not be kicked up so high into the air that the whole foot is visible.

47

You probably decided on a Lhasa Apso as your choice of pet following a visit to the home of a friend or acquaintance, where you saw a well-behaved Apso wandering happily around the house, politely minding his own business. However, as a new owner you must realise that a good deal of care, commitment and careful training goes into raising a boisterous puppy in order for that pup to turn into a well-adjusted adult.

In deciding to take on a new puppy you will be committing yourself to around fourteen years of responsibility, possibly longer. No dog should be discarded after a few months, or even a few years, after the novelty has worn off. Instead, your Lhasa Apso should be joining your household to spend the rest of its days with you.

Temperamentally, a Lhasa Apso can be more difficult to look after than many other breeds, so you will need to carry out a certain amount of training. However, unlike some of the larger guarding breeds, it will not respond well to overly strict

training. Instead, you will need to take a firm but gentle approach in order to get the very best out of your pet.

A Lhasa Apso generally likes to be clean around the house, but you will need to teach your puppy what is and is not expected. You will need to be consistent in your instructions; it is no good accepting certain behaviour one day and not the next. Not only will your puppy simply not understand, he will be utterly confused. Your Lhasa Apso will want to please you, so you will need to demonstrate clearly how he should go about doing this.

Although the dog you are taking into your home will be fairly small, and in this regard less troublesome than a large dog, there will undoubtedly be a period of settling in. This will be great fun, but you must be prepared for mishaps around the home during the first few weeks of your lives together. It will be important that precious ornaments are kept well out of harm's way, and you will have to think twice about where you place hot cups of coffee or anything breakable. Accidents can and do happen, so you will need to think ahead so as to avoid these. Electric cables must be carefully concealed, and your puppy must be taught where he may and where he may not go.

Before making your commitment to a new puppy, do also think carefully about your future holiday plans. Depending on the country in which you live, your dog may or may not be able to travel abroad with you. Because of quarantine laws, no dog can travel freely in and out of Britain and this must be borne in mind ahead of your purchase. If you have thought things through carefully and discussed the matter thoroughly with all of the members of your immediate family, hopefully you will have come to the right decision. If you decide that a Lhasa Apso should join your family, this will hopefully be a happy long-term relationship for all parties concerned.

BUYING A LHASA APSO PUPPY
Although you may be looking for a Lhasa Apso as a pet, rather than as a show dog, this does not mean that you want a dog that is in any way 'second-rate.' A caring breeder will have brought up the entire litter of puppies with the same amount of dedication, and a puppy destined for a pet home

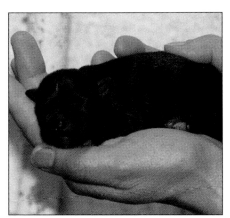

A tiny puppy is a huge responsibility. A breeder puts in a lot of energy to raise pups from day one, and wants to ensure that their pups only go to the best homes.

DID YOU KNOW?

Unfortunately, when a puppy is bought by someone who does not take into consideration the time and attention that dog ownership requires, it is the puppy who suffers when he is either abandoned or placed in a shelter by a frustrated owner. So all of the 'homework' you do in preparation for your pup's arrival will benefit you both. The more informed you are, the more you will know what to expect and the better equipped you will be to handle the ups and downs of raising a puppy. Hopefully, everyone in the household is willing to do his part in raising and caring for the pup. The anticipation of owning a dog often brings a lot of promises from excited family members: 'I will walk him every day,' 'I will feed him,' 'I will housebreak him,' etc., but these things take time and effort, and promises can easily be forgotten once the novelty of the new pet has worn off.

should be just as healthy as one that hopes to end up in the show ring.

Because you have carefully selected this breed, you will want a Lhasa Apso that is a typical specimen, both in looks and in temperament. In your endeavours to find such a puppy, you will have to select the breeder with care. The Kennel Club will almost certainly be able to give you names of contacts within Lhasa Apso breed clubs. These people can possibly put you in touch with breeders who may have puppies for sale. However, although they can point you in the right direction, it will be up to you to do your homework carefully.

Even though you are probably not looking for a show dog, it is always a good idea to visit a show

DID YOU KNOW?

Your selection of a good puppy can be determined by your needs. A show potential or a good pet? It is your choice. Every puppy, however, should be of good temperament. Although show-quality puppies are bred and raised with emphasis on physical conformation, responsible breeders strive for equally good temperament. Do not buy from a breeder who concentrates solely on physical beauty at the expense of personality.

DID YOU KNOW?

You should not even think about buying a puppy that looks sick, undernourished, overly frightened or nervous. Sometimes a timid puppy will warm up to you after a 30-minute 'let's-get-acquainted' session.

so that you can see quality specimens of the breed. This will also give you an opportunity to meet breeders who will probably be able to answer some of your queries. In addition, you will get some idea about which breeders appear to take the best care of their stock and which are likely to have given their puppies the best possible start in life. Something else you may be able to decide upon is which colour appeals to you most, although this is purely personal preference.

When buying your puppy you will need to know about vaccinations, both those already given and those still due. It is important that any injections already given by a veterinary surgeon are documented in writing. A worming routine is also vital for any young puppy, so the breeder should be able to tell you exactly what treatment has been given, when it was administered and how you should continue.

Clearly, when selecting a puppy, the one you choose must

Three Apso puppies with three different personalities. Can you select the best puppy for you just by looking at them? It's best to watch the pups in action before making a choice.

be in good condition. The coat should look healthy and there should be no discharge from the eyes or nose. Ears should also be clean, and of course there should be absolutely no sign of parasites. The pup's skin should be clean and healthy-looking, with no

indication of a rash. Of course, the puppy you choose should not have evidence of loose or otherwise irregular bowel movements.

As in several other breeds, some Lhasa Apso puppies have umbilical hernias. An umbilical hernia can be a seen as a small lump on the tummy where the umbilical cord was attached. It is preferable not to have such a hernia on any puppy, so you should check for this at the outset. If a hernia is present, you should discuss the severity of the problem with the breeder. Most umbilical hernias are safe, but your vet should keep an eye on it in case surgery is needed.

Finally, a few words of advice: find out as much about your

DID YOU KNOW?

Your puppy should have a well-fed appearance but not a distended abdomen, which may indicate worms or incorrect feeding, or both. The body should be firm, with a solid feel. The skin of the abdomen should be pale pink and clean, without signs of scratching or rash. Check the hind legs to make certain that dewclaws were removed, if any were present at birth.

prospective pup's background as you can. Don't be afraid to ask questions of the breeder. Always insist that you see the puppy's dam and, if possible, the sire. While frequently the sire will not be owned by the breeder of the litter, a photograph may be available for you to see. Ask if the breeder has any other of the puppy's relations that you could

DID YOU KNOW?

Two important documents you will get from the breeder are the pup's pedigree and registration papers. The breeder should register the litter and each pup with The Kennel Club, and it is necessary for you to have the paperwork if you plan on showing or breeding in the future.

Make sure you know the breeder's intentions on which type of registration he will obtain for the pup. There are limited registrations which may prohibit the dog from being shown or from competing in non-conformation trials such as Working or Agility if the breeder feels that the pup is not of sufficient quality to do so. There is also a type of registration that will permit the dog in non-conformation competition only.

If your dog is registered with a Kennel-Club-recognised breed club, then you can register the pup with The Kennel Club yourself. Your breeder can assist you with the specifics of the registration process.

meet. For example, there may be an older half-sister or brother, and it would be interesting for you to see how they have turned out— their eventual size, coat quality, temperament and so on.

Be sure, too, that if you decide to buy a puppy, all relevant documentation is provided at the time of sale. You will need a copy of the pedigree, preferably Kennel Club registration documents, vaccination certificates and a feeding chart so that you know exactly how the puppy has been

a Lhasa Apso, which means that you have decided which characteristics you want in a dog and what type of dog will best fit into your family and lifestyle. If you have selected a breeder, you have gone a step further—you have done your research and found a responsible, conscientious person who breeds quality Lhasa Apsos and who should be a reliable source of help as you and your puppy adjust to life together. If you have observed a litter in action, you have obtained a firsthand look at the dynamics of a puppy 'pack' and, thus, you should learn about each pup's individual personality—perhaps you have even found one that particularly appeals to you.

However, even if you have not yet found the Lhasa Apso puppy of your

Pups should stay with their dam until they are at least 12 weeks old. Breeders will not allow the puppies to leave their dam until they have been weaned.

fed and how you should continue. Some careful breeders provide their puppy buyers with a small amount of food. This prevents the risk of an upset tummy, allowing for a gradual change of diet if that particular brand of food is not locally available.

COMMITMENT OF OWNERSHIP
After considering all of these factors, you have most likely already made some very important decisions about selecting your puppy. You have chosen

DID YOU KNOW?

Breeders rarely release puppies until they are eight to ten weeks of age. This is an acceptable age for most breeds of dog, excepting toy breeds which are not released until around 12 weeks, given their petite sizes. If a breeder has a puppy that is 12 weeks or more, it is likely well socialised and housetrained. Be sure that it is otherwise healthy before deciding to take it home.

Litter brother (left) and litter sister (right). Even at this young age one can clearly differentiate between dog and bitch.

dreams, observing pups will help you learn to recognise certain behaviour and to determine what a pup's behaviour indicates about his temperament. You will be able to pick out which pups are the leaders, which ones are less outgoing, which ones are confident, which ones are shy, playful, friendly, aggressive, etc. Equally as important, you will learn to recognise what a healthy pup should look and act like. All of these things will help you in your search, and when you find the Lhasa Apso that was meant for you, you will know it!

Researching your breed, selecting a responsible breeder and observing as many pups as possible are all important steps on the way to dog ownership. It may seem like a lot of effort...and you have not even brought the pup

DID YOU KNOW?

If you lead an erratic, unpredictable life, with daily or weekly changes in your work requirements, consider the problems of owning a puppy. The new puppy has to be fed regularly, socialised (loved, petted, handled, introduced to other people) and, most importantly, allowed to visit outdoors for toilet training. As the dog gets older, it can be more tolerant of deviations in its feeding and toilet relief.

home yet! Remember, though, you cannot be too careful when it comes to deciding on the type of dog you want and finding out about your prospective pup's background. Buying a puppy is not—or should not be—just another whimsical purchase. This is one instance in which you actually do get to choose your own family! You may be thinking that buying a puppy should be fun—it should not be so serious and so much work. Keep in mind that your puppy is not a cuddly stuffed toy or decorative lawn ornament, but a creature that will become a real member of your family. You will come to realise that, whilst buying a puppy is a pleasurable and exciting endeavour, it is not something to be taken lightly. Relax…the fun will start when the pup comes home!

Always keep in mind that a puppy is nothing more than a baby in a furry disguise…a baby who is virtually helpless in a human world and who trusts his owner for fulfilment of his basic needs for survival. In addition to water and shelter, your pup needs care, protection, guidance and love. If you are not prepared to commit to this, then you are not prepared to own a dog.

Wait a minute, you say. How hard could this be? All of my neighbours own dogs and they seem to be doing just fine. Why should I have to worry about all

of this? Well, you should not worry about it; in fact, you will probably find that once your Lhasa Apso pup gets used to his new home, he will fall into his place in the family quite naturally. But it never hurts to emphasise the commitment of dog ownership. With some time and patience, it is really not too difficult to raise a curious and exuberant Lhasa Apso pup to be a well-adjusted and well-mannered adult dog—a dog that could be your most loyal friend.

PREPARING PUPPY'S PLACE IN YOUR HOME
Researching your breed and finding a breeder are only two

Modhish Inky Winki Spida is the proud mother with her newly born litter. Note the guard rail inside the whelping box.

DID YOU KNOW?

If the breeder from whom you are buying a puppy asks you a lot of personal questions, do not be insulted. Such a breeder wants to be sure that you will be a fit provider for his puppy.

You must prepare your home for your Lhasa Apso. Areas in which the dog is allowed should be clearly defined; baby gates or the like can be used to keep him out of areas that are off limits.

aspects of the 'homework' you will have to do before bringing your Lhasa Apso puppy home. You will also have to prepare your home and family for the new addition. Much as you would prepare a nursery for a newborn baby, you will need to designate a place in your home that will be the puppy's own. How you prepare your home will depend on how much freedom the dog will be allowed. Will he be confined to one room or a specific area in the house, or will he be allowed to roam as he pleases? Whatever you decide, you must ensure that he has a place that he can 'call his own.'

When you bring your new puppy into your home, you are bringing him into what will become his home as well. Obviously, you did not buy a puppy so that he could take over your house, but in order for a puppy to grow into a stable, well-

DID YOU KNOW?

The cost of food must also be mentioned. All dogs need a good quality food with an adequate supply of protein to develop their bones and muscles properly. Most dogs are not picky eaters but unless fed properly they can quickly succumb to skin problems.

adjusted dog, he has to feel comfortable in his surroundings. Remember, he is leaving the warmth and security of his mother and littermates, as well as the familiarity of the only place he has ever known, so it is important to make his transition as easy as possible. By preparing a place in your home for the puppy, you are making him feel as welcome as possible in a strange new place. It should not take him long to get used to it, but the sudden shock of being transplanted is somewhat traumatic for a young pup. Imagine how a small child would feel in the same situation—that is how your puppy must be feeling. It is up to you to reassure him and to let him know, 'Little fellow, you are going to like it here!'

WHAT YOU SHOULD BUY
CRATE
To someone unfamiliar with the use of crates in dog training, it may seem like punishment to shut a dog in a crate, but this is not the case at all. Crates are not cruel—crates have many humane and highly effective uses in dog care and training. For example, crate training is a very popular and

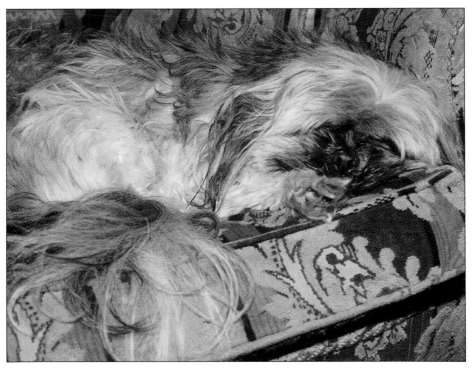

An elderly Lhasa Apso enjoys a nap on his master's favourite chair. Are you prepared to care for your dog through all stages of life?

Your local pet shop probably has a fine array of crates. Buy a crate that will be suitable for a Lhasa Apso both as a puppy and fully grown.

The wire crate has the advantages of being easier to clean, allowing the dog more contact with the people around him and costing less than a fibreglass crate.

PHOTO COURTESY OF DOSKOCIL

for your dog. Like his ancestors, he too will seek out the comfort and retreat of a den—you just happen to be providing him with a safe, clean place to call his own.

As far as purchasing a crate, the type that you buy is up to you. It will most likely be one of the two most popular types: wire or fibreglass. There are advantages and disadvantages to each type. For example, a wire crate is more open, allowing the air to flow through and affording the dog a view of what is going on around him, whilst a fibreglass crate is

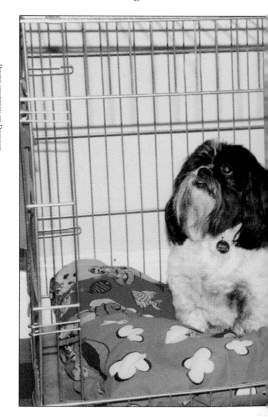

very successful housebreaking method. A crate can keep your dog safe during travel; and, perhaps most importantly, a crate provides your dog with a place of his own in your home. It serves as a 'doggie bedroom' of sorts—your Lhasa Apso can curl up in his crate when he wants to sleep or when he just needs a break. Many dogs sleep in their crates overnight. When lined with soft blankets and a favourite toy, a crate becomes a cosy pseudo-den

sturdier. Both can double as trvel crates, providing protection for the dog. The size of the crate is another thing to consider. Puppies do not stay puppies forever but Lhasa Apsos do not increase too greatly in size so you should easily be able to select a crate that will last into adulthood.

BEDDING

Veterinary bedding in the dog's crate will help the dog feel more at home and you may also pop in a small blanket.

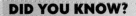

A typical Lhasa Apso whose home is in the Himalayas.

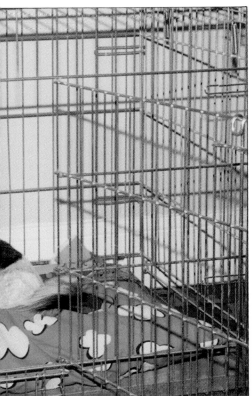

DID YOU KNOW?

During crate training, you should partition off the section of the crate in which the pup stays. If he is given too big an area, this will hinder your training efforts. Crate training is based on the fact that a dog does not like to soil his sleeping quarters, so it is ineffective to keep a pup in a crate that is so big that he can eliminate in one end and get far enough away from it to sleep. Also, you want to make the crate den-like for the pup. Blankets and a favourite toy will make the crate cosy for the small pup; as he grows, you may want to evict some of his 'roommates' to make more room.

It will take some coaxing at first, but be patient. Given some time to get used to it, your pup will adapt to his new home-within-a-home quite nicely.

This will take the place of the leaves, twigs, etc., that the pup would use in the wild to make a den; the pup can make his own 'burrow' in the crate. Although your pup is far removed from his den-making ancestors, the denning instinct is still a part of his genetic makeup. Secondly, until you bring your pup home, he has been sleeping amidst the warmth of his mother and litter-mates, and whilst a blanket is not the same as a warm, breathing body, it still provides heat and something with which to snuggle. You will want to wash your pup's blankets frequently in case he has an accident in his crate, and replace or remove any blanket that becomes ragged and starts to fall apart.

Toys

Toys are a must for dogs of all ages, especially for curious playful pups. Puppies are the 'children' of the dog world, and what child does not love toys? Chew toys provide enjoyment to both dog and owner—your dog will enjoy playing with his favourite toys, whilst you will enjoy the fact that they distract him from your expensive shoes and leather sofa. Puppies love to chew; in fact, chewing is a physical need for pups as they are teething, and everything looks appetising! The full range of your possessions—

The garden should be secure so the Apso can go out to relieve himself and enjoy supervised free play without the danger of his getting loose.

PHOTO COURTESY OF MIKKI PET PRODUCTS

Your local pet shop probably has a wide variety of toys made especially for dogs. Never use toys intended for humans as they are too easily torn apart by a dog's sharp teeth.

from old dishcloth to Oriental rug—are fair game in the eyes of a teething pup. Puppies are not all that discerning when it comes to finding something to literally 'sink their teeth into'—everything tastes great!

Lhasa Apso puppies are fairly aggressive chewers and only the hardest, strongest toys should be offered to them. Breeders advise owners to resist stuffed toys, because they can become de-stuffed in no time. The overly excited pup may ingest the stuffing, which is neither digestible nor nutritious.

Similarly, squeaky toys are quite popular, but must be

DID YOU KNOW?

With a big variety of dog toys available, and so many that look like they would be a lot of fun for a dog, be careful in your selection. It is amazing what a set of puppy teeth can do to an innocent-looking toy, so, obviously, safety is a major consideration. Be sure to choose the most durable products that you can find. Hard nylon bones and toys are a safe bet, and many of them are offered in different scents and flavours that will be sure to capture your dog's attention. It is always fun to play a game of catch with your dog, and there are balls and flying discs that are specially made to withstand dog teeth.

61

avoided for the Lhasa Apso. Perhaps a squeaky toy can be used as an aid in training, but not for free play. If a pup 'disembowels' one of these, the small plastic squeaker inside can be dangerous if swallowed. Monitor the condition of all your pup's toys carefully and get rid of any that have been chewed to the point of becoming potentially dangerous.

Be careful of natural bones, which have a tendency to splinter into sharp, dangerous pieces. Also be careful of rawhide, which can turn into pieces that are easy to swallow or into a mushy mess on your carpet.

LEAD

A nylon lead is probably the best option as it is the most resistant to

Most trainers recommend using a light-weight nylon lead for your Lhasa Apso. Pet shops offer dozens of choices for collars ans leads, in different styles, colours and lengths.

puppy teeth should your pup take a liking to chewing on his lead. Of course, this is a habit that should be nipped in the bud, but if your pup likes to chew on his lead he has a very slim chance of being able to chew through the strong nylon. Nylon leads are also lightweight, which is good for a young Lhasa Apso who is just getting used to the idea of walking on a lead. For everyday walking and safety purposes, the nylon lead is a good choice. As your pup grows up and gets used to walking on the lead, you may want to purchase a flexible lead. These leads allow you to extend the length to give the dog a broader area to explore or to shorten the length to keep the

The **BUCKLE COLLAR** is the standard collar used for everyday purpose. Be sure that you adjust the buckle on growing puppies. Check it every day. It can become too tight overnight! These collars can be made of leather or nylon. Attach your dog's identification tags to this collar.

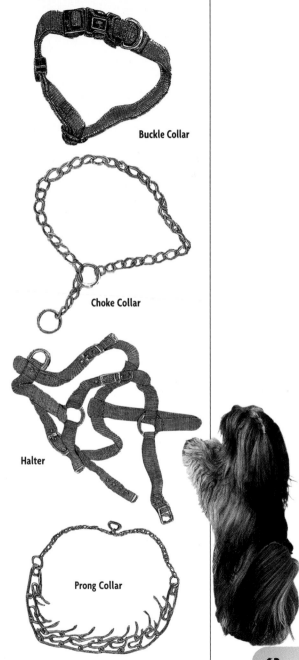

Buckle Collar

The **CHOKE CHAIN** is the usual collar recommended for training. It is constructed of highly polished steel so that it slides easily through the stainless steel loop. The idea is that the dog controls the pressure around its neck and he will stop pulling if the collar becomes uncomfortable. Never leave a choke collar on your dog when not training.

Choke Collar

The **HALTER** is for a trained dog that has to be restrained to prevent running away, chasing a cat and the like. Considered the most humane of all collars, it is frequently used on smaller dogs for which collars are not comfortable.

Halter

The **PRONG COLLAR** certainly appears ominous, like an ancient instrument of torture. Although it is not intended to 'torture' a dog, it is only recommended on the most difficult of dogs, and never on small dogs. It should only be employed by someone who knows how to use it properly.

Prong Collar

63

Quality dog bowls are made from stainess steel, pottery or heavy plastic.

close to you. Choke, prong or other heavy training collars are never recommended for use on small dogs like the Lhasa Apso. They are not necessary and can cause the dog injury.

COLLAR
Your pup should get used to wearing a collar all the time since you will want to attach his ID tags to it. You have to attach the lead to something! A lightweight nylon collar is a good choice; make sure that it fits snugly enough so that the pup cannot wriggle out of it, but is loose enough so that it will not be uncomfortably tight around the pup's neck. You should be able to fit a finger between

Tying the Apso's head furnishings back will avoid soiling the hair when he eats or takes a drink.

the pup and the collar. It may take some time for your pup to get used to wearing the collar, but soon he will not even notice that it is there. Choke collars are made for training, but should only be used by an experienced handler.

FOOD AND WATER BOWLS
Your pup will need two bowls, one for food and one for water. You may want two sets of bowls, one for inside and one for outside, depending on where the dog will be fed and where he will be spending most of his time. Stainless steel or sturdy plastic bowls are popular choices. Plastic bowls are more chewable. Dogs tend not to chew on the steel variety, which can be sterilised. It is important to buy sturdy bowls since anything is in danger of being chewed by puppy teeth and you do not want your dog to be constantly chewing apart his bowl (for his safety and for your purse!).

CLEANING SUPPLIES
Until a pup is housetrained you will be doing a lot of cleaning.

PHOTO COURTESY OF MIKKI PET PRODUCTS

Responsible, law-abiding dog owners pick up their dogs' dropping whenever they are in public. Pooper-scooper devices make the job quick and easy.

Accidents will occur, which is okay in the beginning because the puppy does not know any better. All you can do is be prepared to clean up any 'accidents.' Old rags, towels, newspapers and a safe disinfectant are good to have on hand.

Your local pet shop will probably have a wide range of food and water bowls.

BEYOND THE BASICS
The items previously discussed are the bare necessities. You will find out what else you need as you go along—grooming supplies, flea/tick protection, baby gates to partition a room, etc. These things will vary depending on your situation but it is important that you have everything you need to feed and make your Lhasa Apso comfortable in his first few days at home.

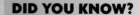

Get everything you need BEFORE you bring your new puppy home. Your puppy's first night in his new home will be memorable for both you and the puppy.

PUPPY-PROOFING YOUR HOME

Aside from making sure that your Lhasa Apso will be comfortable in your home, you also have to make sure that your home is safe for your Lhasa Apso. This means taking precautions that your pup will not get into anything he should not get into and that there is nothing within his reach that may harm him should he sniff it, chew it, inspect it, etc. This probably seems obvious since, whilst you are primarily concerned with your pup's safety, at the same time you do not want your belongings to be ruined. Breakables should be placed out of reach if your dog is to have full run of the house. If he is to be limited to certain places within the house, keep any potentially dangerous items in the 'off-limits' areas. An electrical cord can pose a danger should the puppy decide to taste it—and who is going to convince a pup that it would not make a great chew toy? Cords should be fastened tightly against the wall. If your dog is going to spend time in a crate, make sure that there is nothing near his crate that he can reach if he sticks his curious little nose or paws

Lhasa Apsos, when properly fed and cared for, stay in remarkable condition through-out their lives. This youthful-looking Apso is 12 years old and looking like a pup!

through the openings. Just as you would with a child, keep all household cleaners and chemicals where the pup cannot get to them.

It is also important to make sure that the outside of your home is safe. Of course your puppy should never be unsupervised, but a pup let loose in the garden will want to run and explore, and he should be granted that freedom. Do not let a fence give you a false sense of security; you would be surprised how crafty (and persistent) a dog can be in figuring out how to dig under and squeeze his way through small holes, or to jump or climb over a fence. The remedy is to make the fence high enough so that it really is impossible for your dog to get over it (about 3 metres should

suffice), and well embedded into the ground. Be sure to repair or secure any gaps in the fence. Check the fence periodically to ensure that it is in good shape and make repairs as needed; a very determined pup may return to the same spot to 'work on it' until he is able to get through.

DID YOU KNOW?

Scour your carport for potential puppy dangers. Remove weed killers, pesticides and antifreeze materials. Antifreeze is highly toxic and even a few drops can kill an adult dog. The sweet taste attracts the animal, who will quickly consume it from the floor or curbside.

FIRST TRIP TO THE VET

You have picked out your puppy, and your home and family are ready. Now all you have to do is collect your Lhasa Apso from the breeder and the fun begins, right? Well…not so fast. Something else you need to prepare is your pup's first trip to the veterinary surgeon. Perhaps the breeder can recommend someone in the area that specialises in Lhasa Apsos, or maybe you know some other Lhasa Apso owners who can suggest a good vet. Either way, you should have an appointment arranged for your pup before you pick him up and plan on taking him for an examination before bringing him home.

The pup's first visit will consist of

DID YOU KNOW?

Taking your dog from the breeder to your home in a car can be a very uncomfortable experience for both of you. The puppy will have been taken from his warm, friendly, safe environment and brought into a strange new environment. An environment that moves! Be prepared for loose bowels, urination, crying, whining and even fear biting. With proper love and encouragement when you arrive home, the stress of the trip should quickly disappear.

DID YOU KNOW?

It will take at least two weeks for your puppy to become accustomed to his new surroundings. Give him lots of love, attention, handling, frequent opportunities to relieve himself, a diet he likes to eat and a place he can call his own.

an overall examination to make sure that the pup does not have any problems that are not apparent to the eye. The veterinary surgeon will also set up a schedule for the pup's vaccinations; the breeder will inform you of which ones the pup has already received and the vet can continue from there.

INTRODUCTION TO THE FAMILY

Everyone in the house will be excited about the puppy coming home and will want to pet him and play with him, but it is best to make the introduction low-key so as not to overwhelm the puppy. He is apprehensive already. It is the first time he has been separated from his mother and the breeder, and the ride to your home is likely the first time he has been in an auto. The last thing you want to do is smother him, as this will only frighten him further. This is not to say that human contact is not extremely necessary at this stage, because this is the time when a connection between the pup and his human family is formed. Gentle petting and soothing words should help console him, as well as just putting him down and letting him explore on his own (under your watchful eye, of course).

A basket with veterinary bedding is an excellent choice for the new puppy. Offer the puppy a safe chew toy to take to his new bed.

The pup may approach the family members or may busy himself with exploring for a while. Gradually, each person should spend some time with the pup, one at a time, crouching down to get as close to the pup's level as possible and letting him sniff their hands and petting him gently. He definitely needs human attention and he needs to be touched—this is how to form an immediate bond. Just remember that the pup is experiencing a lot of things for the first time, at the same time. There are new people, new noises, new smells, and new things to investigate: so be gentle, be affectionate, and be as comforting as you can be.

YOUR PUP'S FIRST NIGHT HOME

You have travelled home with your new charge safely in his basket or crate. He's been to the vet for a thorough check-over; he's been weighed, his papers examined; perhaps he's even been vaccinated and wormed as well. He's met the family, licked the whole family, including the excited children and the less-than-happy cat. He's explored his area, his new bed, the garden and anywhere else he's been permitted. He's eaten his first meal at home and relieved himself in the proper place. He's heard lots of new sounds, smelled new friends and seen more of the outside world than ever before.

That was just the first day! He's worn out and is ready for bed...or so you think!

It's puppy's first night and you

DID YOU KNOW?

Training your puppy takes much patience and can be frustrating at times, but you should see results from your efforts. If you have a puppy that seems untrainable, take him to a trainer or behaviourist. The dog may have a personality problem that requires the help of a professional, or perhaps you need help in learning how to train your dog.

69

are ready to say 'Good night'—keep in mind that this is puppy's first night ever to be sleeping alone. His dam and littermates are no longer at paw's length and he's a bit scared, cold and lonely. Be reassuring to your new family member. This is not the time to spoil him and give in to his inevitable whining.

Puppies whine. They whine to let the others know where they are and hopefully to get company out of it. Place your pup in his new bed or crate in his room and close the door. Mercifully, he may fall asleep without a peep. If the inevitable occurs, ignore the whining: he is fine. Be strong and keep his interest in mind. Do not allow your heart to become guilty and visit the pup. He will fall asleep.

Many breeders recommend placing a piece of bedding from his former homestead in his new bed so that he recognises the scent of his littermates. Others still advise placing a hot water bottle in his bed for warmth. This latter may be a good idea provided the pup doesn't attempt to suckle—he'll get good and wet and may not fall asleep so fast.

Puppy's first night can be somewhat stressful for the pup and his new family. Remember that you are setting the tone of nighttime at your house. Unless you want to play with your pup every evening at 10 p.m., midnight and 2 a.m., don't initiate the habit. Your family will thank you, and so will your pup!

PREVENTING PUPPY PROBLEMS
SOCIALISATION
Now that you have done all of the preparatory work and have helped your pup get accustomed to his new home and family, it is about time for you to have some fun! Socialising your Lhasa Apso pup gives you the opportunity to show off your new friend, and your pup gets to reap the benefits of being an adorable furry creature that people will want to pet and, in general, think is absolutely precious!

Besides getting to know his new family, your puppy should be exposed to other people, animals and situations, but of course he must not come into close contact with dogs you don't know well until his course of injections is fully completed. This will help him become well adjusted as he grows up and less prone to being timid or fearful of the new things he will encounter. Your pup's socialisation began at the breeder's but now it is your responsibility to continue it. The socialisation he receives up until the age of 12 weeks is the most critical, as this is the time when he forms his impressions of the outside world. Be especially careful during the eight-to-ten-week period, also known as the

DID YOU KNOW?

Thorough socialisation includes not only meeting new people but also being introduced to new experiences such as riding in the auto, having his coat brushed, hearing the television, walking in a crowd—the list is endless. The more your pup experiences, and the more positive the experiences are, the less of a shock and the less scary it will be for your pup to encounter new things.

fear period. The interaction he receives during this time should be gentle and reassuring. Lack of socialisation can manifest itself in fear and aggression as the dog grows up. He needs lots of human

A happy trio of friends. Apsos get along with dogs of all sizes.

contact, affection, handling and exposure to other animals.

Once your pup has received his necessary vaccinations, feel free to take him out and about (on his lead, of course). Walk him around the neighbourhood, take him on your daily errands, let people pet him, let him meet other dogs and pets, etc. Puppies do not have to try to make friends; there will be no shortage of people who will want to introduce themselves. Just make sure that you carefully supervise each meeting. If the neighbourhood children want to say hello, for example, that is great—children and pups most often make great companions. Sometimes an excited child can unintentionally handle a pup too roughly, or an overzealous pup can playfully nip a little too hard. You want to make socialisation experiences positive ones. What a pup learns during this very formative stage will impact his attitude toward future encounters. You want your dog to be comfort-able around everyone. A pup that has a bad experience with a child may grow up to be a dog that is shy around or aggressive toward children.

CONSISTENCY IN TRAINING

Dogs, being pack animals, naturally need a leader, or else they try to establish dominance in their packs. When you bring a dog into your family, the choice of who becomes the leader and who becomes the 'pack' is entirely up to you! Your pup's intuitive quest for dominance, coupled with the fact that it is nearly impossible to look at an adorable Lhasa Apso pup, with his 'puppy-dog' eyes and not cave in, give the pup almost an unfair advantage in getting the upper hand! A pup will definitely test the waters to see what he can and cannot do. Do not give in to those pleading eyes—stand your ground when it comes to disciplining the pup and make sure that all family members do the same. It will only confuse the pup when Mother tells him to get off the couch when he is used to sitting up there with Father to watch the nightly news. Avoid discrepancies by having all members of the household decide on the rules before the pup even comes home...and be consistent in enforcing them! Early training shapes the dog's personality, so you cannot be unclear in what you expect.

DID YOU KNOW?

An important consideration to be discussed is the sex of your puppy. For a family companion, a bitch may be the better choice, considering the female's inbred concern for all young creatures and her accompanying tolerance and patience. It is always advised to spay a pet bitch, which may guarantee her a longer life.

COMMON PUPPY PROBLEMS

The best way to prevent puppy problems is to be proactive in stopping an undesirable behaviour as soon as it starts. The old saying 'You can't teach an old dog new tricks' does not necessarily hold true, but it is true that it is much easier to discourage bad behaviour in a young developing pup than to wait until the pup's bad behaviour becomes the adult dog's bad habit. There are some problems that are especially prevalent in puppies as they develop.

NIPPING

As puppies start to teethe, they feel the need to sink their teeth into anything available…unfortunately that includes your fingers, arms, hair, and toes. You may find this behaviour cute for the first five seconds…until you feel just how sharp those puppy teeth are. This is something you want to discourage immediately and consistently with a firm 'No!' (or whatever number of firm 'No's' it takes for him to understand that you mean business). Then replace your finger with an appropriate chew toy. Whilst this behaviour is merely annoying when the dog is young, it can become dangerous as your Lhasa Apso's adult teeth grow in and his jaws develop, and he continues to think it is okay to gnaw on human appendages.

CRYING/WHINING

Your pup will often cry, whine, whimper, howl or make some type of commotion when he is left alone. This is basically his way of calling out for attention to make sure that you know he is

DID YOU KNOW?

Chewing goes hand in hand with nipping in the sense that a teething puppy is always looking for a way to soothe his aching gums. In this case, instead of chewing on you, he may have taken a liking to your favourite shoe or something else which he should not be chewing. Again, realise that this is a normal canine behaviour that does not need to be discouraged, only redirected. Your pup just needs to be taught what is acceptable to chew on and what is off limits. Consistently tell him NO when you catch him chewing on something forbidden and give him a chew toy. Conversely, praise him when you catch him chewing on something appropriate. In this way you are discouraging the inappropriate behaviour and reinforcing the desired behaviour. The puppy chewing should stop after his adult teeth have come in, but an adult dog continues to chew for various reasons—perhaps because he is bored, perhaps to relieve tension or perhaps he just likes to chew. That is why it is important to redirect his chewing when he is still young.

A housetrained Apso may not enjoy going out to relieve himself in very cold weather. A specially made doggy sweater can help keep him warm.

Opposite page: Soft, absorbent paper can be used as bedding for very young puppies.

there and that you have not forgotten about him. He feels insecure when he is left alone, when you are out of the house and he is in his crate or when you are in another part of the house and he cannot see you. The noise he is making is an

expression of the anxiety he feels at being alone, so he needs to be taught that being alone is okay. You are not actually training the dog to stop making noise, you are training him to feel comfortable when he is alone and thus removing the need for him to make the noise. This is where the crate filled with cosy bedding and toys comes in handy. You want to know that he is safe when you are not there to supervise, and you know that he will be safe in his crate rather than roaming freely about the house. In order for the pup to stay in his crate without making a fuss, he needs to be comfortable in his crate. On that note, it is extremely important that the crate is never used as a form of punishment, or the pup will have a negative association with the crate.

Accustom the pup to the crate in short, gradually increasing time intervals in which you put him in the crate, maybe with a treat, and stay in the room with him. If he cries or makes a fuss, do not go to him, but stay in his sight. Gradually he will realise that staying in his crate is all right without your help, and it will not be so traumatic for him when you are not around. You may want to leave the radio on softly when you leave the house; the sound of human voices may be comforting to him.

DID YOU KNOW?

The majority of problems that are commonly seen in young pups will disappear as your dog gets older. However, how you deal with problems when he is young will determine how he reacts to discipline as an adult dog. It is important to establish who is boss (hopefully it will be you!) right away when you are first bonding wiith your dog. This bond will set the tone for the rest of your life together.

DIETARY AND FEEDING CONSIDERATIONS

Today the choices of food for your Lhasa Apso are many and varied. There are simply dozens of brands of food in all sorts of flavours and textures, ranging from puppy diets to those for seniors. There are even hypoallergenic and low-calorie diets available. Because your Lhasa Apso's food has a bearing on coat, health and temperament, it is essential that the most suitable diet is selected for a Lhasa Apso of his age. It is fair to say, however, that even dedicated owners can be somewhat perplexed by the enormous range of foods available. Only understanding what is best for your dog will help you reach a valued decision.

Dog foods are produced in three basic types: dried, semi-moist and tinned. Dried foods are useful for the cost-conscious for overall they tend to be less expensive than semi-moist or tinned. These contain the least fat and the most preservatives. In

> ### DID YOU KNOW?
>
> Selecting the best dried dog food is difficult. There is no majority consensus amongst veterinary scientists as to the value of nutrient analyses (protein, fat, fibre, moisture, ash, cholesterol, minerals, etc.). All agree that feeding trials are what matters, but you also have to consider the individual dog. Its weight, age, activity and what pleases its taste, all must be considered. It is probably best to take the advice of your veterinary surgeon. Every dog's dietary requirements vary, even during the lifetime of a particular dog.
>
> If your dog is fed a good dried food, it does not require supplements of meat or vegetables. Dogs do appreciate a little variety in their diets so you may choose to stay with the same brand, but vary the flavour. Alternatively you may wish to add a little flavoured stock to give a difference to the taste.

Lhasa Apso puppies enjoy a milk feed as part of their weaning process.

DID YOU KNOW?

You must store your dry dog food carefully. Open packages of dog food quickly lose their vitamin value, usually within 90 days of being opened. Mould spores and vermin could also contaminate the food.

An Apso bitch during the whelping process. Puppies should instinctively want to suckle and should exhibit this behaviour within moments of birth.

general tinned foods are made up of 60–70 percent water, whilst semi-moist ones often contain so much sugar that they are perhaps the least preferred by owners, even though their dogs seem to like them.

When selecting your dog's diet, three stages of development must be considered: the puppy stage, adult stage and the senior or veteran stage.

PUPPY STAGE

Puppies instinctively want to suck milk from their mother's teats and a normal puppy will exhibit this behaviour from just a few moments following birth. If puppies do not attempt to suckle within the first half-hour or so, they should be encouraged to do so by placing them on a nipple, having selected ones with plenty of milk. This early milk supply is important in providing colostrum to protect the puppies during the first eight to ten weeks of their lives. Although a mother's milk is

much better than any milk formula, despite there being some excellent ones available, if the puppies do not feed you will have to feed them yourself. For those with less experience, advice from a veterinary surgeon is important so that you feed not only the right quantity of milk but that of correct quality, fed at suitably frequent intervals, usually every two hours during the first few days of life.

Puppies should be allowed to nurse from their mothers for about the first six weeks,

DID YOU KNOW?

A good test for proper diet is the colour, odour, and firmness of your dog's stool. A healthy dog usually produces three semi-hard stools per day. The stools should have no unpleasant odour. They should be the same colour from excretion to excretion.

although from the third or fourth week you will have begun to introduce small portions of suitable solid food. Most breeders like to introduce alternate milk and meat meals initially, building up to weaning time.

By the time the puppies are seven or a maximum of eight weeks old, they should be fully weaned and fed solely on a proprietary puppy food. Selection of the most suitable, good-quality diet at this time is essential for a puppy's fastest growth rate is during the first year of life. Veterinary surgeons are usually able to offer advice in this regard and, although the frequency of meals will have been reduced over time, only

when a young dog has reached the age of about 18 months should an adult diet be fed.

Puppy and junior diets should be well balanced for the needs of your dog, so that except in certain circumstances additional vitamins, minerals and proteins will not be required.

ADULT DIETS

A dog is considered an adult when it has stopped growing, so in general the diet of a Lhasa Apso can be changed to an adult one at about 12 months of age. Again you should rely upon your veterinary surgeon or dietary specialist to recommend an acceptable maintenance diet. Major dog food manufacturers specialise in this type of food, and it is just necessary for you to select the one best suited to your dog's needs. Active dogs may have different requirements than sedate dogs.

SENIOR DIETS

As dogs get older, their metabolism changes. The older dog usually exercises less, moves more slowly and sleeps more. This change in lifestyle and physiological performance requires a change in diet. Since these changes take place slowly, they might not be recognisable. What is easily recognisable is weight gain. By continuing to

DID YOU KNOW?

Many adult diets are based on grain. There is nothing wrong with this as long as it does not contain soy meal. Diets based on soy often cause flatulence (passing gas).

Grain-based diets are almost always the least expensive and a good grain diet is just as good as the most expensive diet containing animal protein.

There are many cases, however, when your dog might require a special diet. These special requirements should only be recommended by your veterinary surgeon.

What are you feeding your dog?

Read the label on your dog food. Many dog foods only advise what 50 to 55% of the contents are, leaving the other 45% to doubt.

1.3% Calcium

1.6% Fatty Acids

4.6% Crude Fibre

11% Moisture

14% Crude Fat

22% Crude Protein

45.5% ? ? ?

feed your dog an adult-maintenance diet when it is slowing down metabolically, your dog will gain weight. Obesity in an older dog compounds the health problems that already accompany old age.

As your dog gets older, few of their organs function up to par. The kidneys slow down and the intestines become less efficient. These age-related factors are best handled with a change in diet and a change in feeding schedule to give smaller portions that are more easily digested.

There is no single best diet for every older dog. Whilst many dogs do well on light or senior diets, other dogs do better on puppy diets or other special premium diets such as lamb and rice. Be sensitive to your senior Lhasa Apso's diet and this will help control other problems that may arise with your old friend.

WATER
Just as your dog needs proper nutrition from his food, water is an essential 'nutrient' as well. Water keeps the dog's body properly hydrated and promotes normal function of the body's systems. During housebreaking it is necessary to keep an eye on how much water your Lhasa Apso is drinking, but once he is reliably trained he should have access to clean fresh water at all times. Make sure that the dog's water bowl is clean, and change the water often, making sure that water is always available for your dog, especially if you feed dried food.

EXERCISE
Although a Lhasa Apso is small, all dogs require some form of exercise, regardless of breed. A sedentary lifestyle is as harmful to a dog as it is to a person. The Lhasa Apso is a fairly active breed that enjoys exercise, but you don't have to be an Olympic athlete to give him the activity he needs. Regular walks, play sessions in the garden or letting the dog run free in the garden under your supervision are sufficient forms of exercise for the Lhasa Apso. For those who are more ambitious, you will find that your Lhasa Apso also enjoys long walks, an occasional hike or even a swim! Bear in mind that an overweight dog should never be suddenly over-exercised; instead he should be allowed to increase exercise slowly. Not only is exercise essential to keep the dog's body fit, it is essential to his mental well being. A bored dog will find something to do, which often manifests itself in some type of destructive behaviour. In this sense, it is essential for the owner's mental well-being as well!

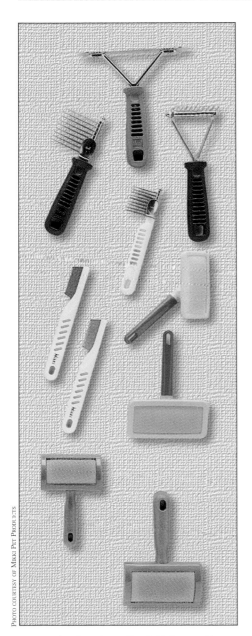

Your local pet shop will probably have a wide assortment of grooming tools to enable you to keep your Apso in perfect form.

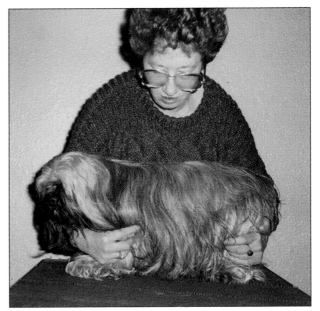

GROOMING

Your Lhasa Apso will need to be groomed regularly, so it is essential that short grooming sessions are introduced from a very early age. From the beginning, a few minutes each day should be set aside. The duration should build up slowly as the puppy matures and the coat grows in length. Your puppy should be taught to stand on a solid surface for grooming—a suitable table on which the dog will not slip. Under no circumstances leave your Apso alone on a table for he may all too easily jump off and injure himself.

When the puppy is used to standing on the table, you will need to teach him to be rolled

The process of putting an Apso over on his side to be groomed begins with grasping the legs and gently rolling him down.

81

over onto his side. This you will do by grasping his front and back legs on the opposite side of your own body, then gently placing him down by leaning over him for reassurance. To begin with, just stroke his tummy so that he looks upon this new routine as something highly pleasurable. Then, when you know he is comfortable with this, introduce a few gentle brush strokes. Be sure you don't tug at any knots at this stage, for this would cause him to associate the grooming routine with pain. This may take a little getting used to both for you and your puppy, but only if your

Apso learns to lie down on his side will you easily be able to groom in all the awkward places. You will both be glad you had a little patience to learn this trick from the very start!

You will notice that not only does your Lhasa Apso's coat grow longer with age but also, usually between 10 and 12 months, the coat changes from a puppy coat to an adult one. This will be a difficult time when knots will form very easily, and you will realise how comparatively easy it is to groom the puppy coat!

You will certainly need to groom the coat between bath times, but never groom the coat when completely dry. To avoid breaking the ends, use a light conditioning spray; even water dispensed from a fine-spray bottle is better than no moisture at all.

ROUTINE GROOMING

With your Lhasa Apso lying on his side, the coat should be parted, layered and brushed section by section, always in the direction of the coat growth. It is imperative to groom right down to the skin so that the undercoat is not left matted. After using a good-quality bristle brush, a wide-toothed comb can be used to finish each section.

If you do find matts in your Apso's coat, spray the matt with

DID YOU KNOW?

How much grooming equipment you purchase will depend on how much grooming you are going to do. Here are some basics:
- Natural bristle brush
- Metal comb
- Scissors
- Blaster
- Rubber mat
- Dog shampoo
- Conditioner
- Conditioning spray
- Dental elastics
- Spray hose attachment
- Ear cleaner
- Cotton buds
- Ear tweezers
- Towels
- Nail clippers

Healthy dog hairs enlarged about 500 times their natural size. The inset shows a growing tip. Scanning electron micrographs by Dr. Dennis Kunkel, University of Hawaii.

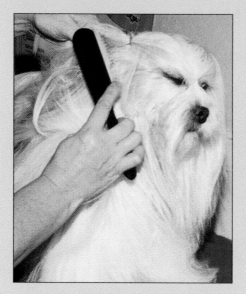

Brushing the coat thoroughly gets out any matts and tangles. Brushing is necessary both before bathing and after the coat is completely dry.

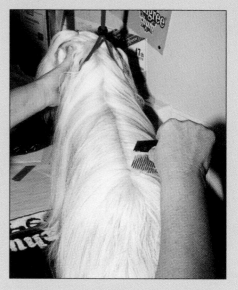

A straight part is made, starting at the dog's head and running the entire length of the back.

Combing follows brushing, using a fine-toothed metal comb.

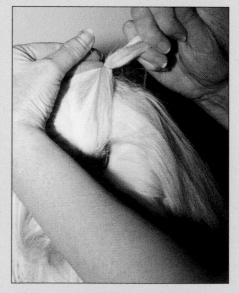

The hair is tied back on each side with a light rubber-band, taking care not to pull the hair too tightly.

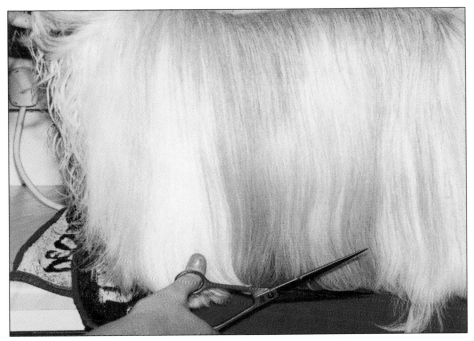

The hair is trimmed uniformly at ground level, using the grooming table as a guide.

a generous amount of conditioning or anti-tangle spray. Leave this to soak in for a few moments, then gently tease out the matt with your fingers. Always work from the inside out, or the knot will just get tighter! Tight knots will probably need to be teased out using a wide-toothed comb, but don't tug at the knot for this will be painful and will also take out too much coat.

Take care grooming the tummy and under the 'armpits,' for these areas are especially sensitive. There is really no harm in cutting away small tight knots from under the armpits, as these will not show and the dog

All of the grooming effort pays off when you see the results: a Lhasa Apso with a beautiful coat.

The hair should be removed from in between the foot pads to avoid uncomfortable hairballs from forming.

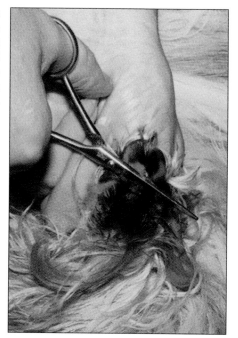

will feel more comfortable.

Because a Lhasa Apso's coat just seems to keep on growing, it is usually necessary to trim the coat at ground level. To do this neatly, stand your dog on the edge of a table and, using hairdressing scissors, carefully cut off the hair that hangs below the edge of the table. This will leave a nice straight line around the bottom of the coat. Trimming below the pads of the feet prevents uncomfortable hairballs forming between the pads. On males, most owners also trim of a little hair from the end of the penis, but a good half inch or a few centimetres must be left so that tiny hairs to not aggravate

the penis and set up infection. Whatever you do, take care not to cut through a nipple—and remember that males have little nipples too!

Legs and trousers of a Lhasa Apso are very heavily coated, so will also need regular grooming. To prevent knots and tangles, be sure to immediately remove any debris that may have accumulated following a visit outdoors. Also always check your dog's back end to see that nothing remains attached to the coat from his toilet. Between baths you may like to use a damp sponge, but always be sure to dry the coat thoroughly. Drying will keep your Apso comfortable and will prevent the coat from curling too much.

Some Lhasa Apsos don't seem to mind having their feet groomed, others hate it. Nonetheless, you will have to check feet thoroughly on a regular basis. Be sure you don't allow knots to build up between the toes, and always keep an eye on the length of the toenails.

THE HEAD
AND THE FINISHING TOUCHES

It is essential to keep whiskers, beard and eyes of a Lhasa Apso clean, so these must be checked every day. Eyes can be cleaned with a canine liquid eye cleaner. Beard and whiskers can be washed and combed through, and some owners find it useful to attach elastic on each side of the beard to prevent soiling, especially when the dog is eating.

When grooming, pay special attention to the hair behind the ear—this is often of a finer texture and knots easily. When not in the show ring, owners often like to tie the head hair into tiny elastic bands on each side of the head. Most owners use dental elastics, but take care not to pull up the hair too tightly so that it pulls on the eyes. Elastics will generally need to be changed at least once a day. Never pull them out; always cut them carefully with scissors so as not to damage any hair. Under no circumstances should the head hair be trimmed for the show ring although, if a Lhasa Apso is maintained in pet trim, the head hair can be cut short to match the rest of the coat. Some pet owners, though, like to keep long fringing on the ears.

When grooming is complete, take a wide-toothed comb to create a straight parting down the length of the back so that the coat falls evenly on either side.

BATHING AND DRYING
How frequently you decide to bathe your Lhasa Apso will depend very much on whether your dog is a show dog or a pet. Show dogs are usually bathed

The coat is thoroughly saturated with lukewarm water.

Dog shampoo is applied to the dog's coat.

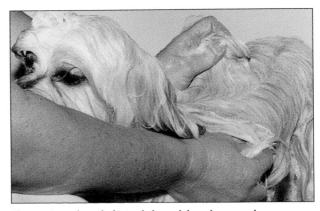

Shampoo is gently worked into a lather and the suds massaged all the way to the skin.

All of the hard-to-reach places should be thoroughly cleaned.

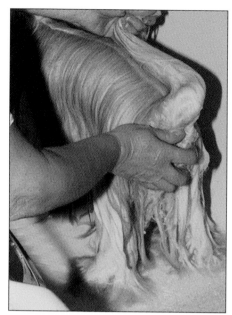

After the dog is rinsed, he is wrapped in a soft towel and lifted from the tub.

before every show, which may be as frequent as once a week. Pet dogs are usually bathed less frequently, especially if they are kept in puppy trim because the coat does not drag on the ground to pick up dirt and debris.

Every owner has his or her own preference as to how best to bathe, but ideally the coat should have been groomed through before bathing. I like to stand my own dogs on a non-slip mat in the bath, then wet the coat thoroughly using a shower. It is imperative that the water temperature previously has been tested on your own hand. Use a good-quality shampoo designed especially for dogs, always stroking it into the coat rather than rubbing, so as not to create knots. When this has been thoroughly rinsed out, apply a canine conditioner in the same manner, then rinse again until the water runs clear. Many people like to use a baby shampoo on the head to avoid irritation to the eyes, and some like to plug the ears with cotton wool to avoid water getting inside. Personally, I use neither of these; instead I just take special care in that area, and I have never encountered problems.

Before taking your dog out of the bath, it is a good idea to use a highly absorbent cloth to soak up excess moisture. Remove

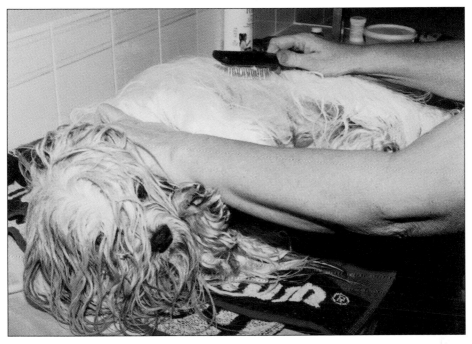

Post-bath brushing on the grooming table is done while using a hair dryer to keep the coat free of tangles while drying.

your Apso from the bath by wrapping him in a clean towel and lifting him out. Undoubtedly your dog will want to shake—so be prepared!

Drying can be done on whichever table you use for the grooming process. Work systematically, all the while brushing as well as applying warm air from the hair dryer.

Never just blow-dry the dog with the intention of grooming later, or your Lhasa Apso's coat will not end up looking in good condition. Certainly never allow an Apso to dry naturally.

Put the finishing touches to your dog's coat, just as you would have done if grooming

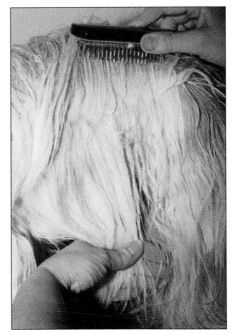

Brush the hair in the direction in which it lays.

Cleaning an Apso's ears on a regular basis is very important. Use an ear cleansing solution (available from your vet or pet shop) or specially made cleaning wipes. Always be on the lookout for ear mites or infection.

The long hairs growing in the Apso's ears should be removed by pulling only a few hairs at a time. This is painless if it is done properly.

without a bath. Bathing and grooming a long-coated breed is always a lengthy task but, I assure you, the end result will make it all worthwhile.

EAR CLEANING

Because the Lhasa Apso has such a long coat, long hair will also grow inside the ears. This should carefully be plucked out either with special blunt-ended tweezers or, if you prefer, with your fingertips. By always removing only a few hairs at a time, the procedure should be entirely painless.

Ears should be kept clean. This can be done with a cotton wipe and special cleaner or ear powder made especially for dogs. Be on the lookout for any signs of infection or ear mite infestation. If your Lhasa Apso has been shaking his head or scratching at his ears frequently, this usually indicates a problem. If his ears have an unusual odour, this is a sure sign of mite infestation or infection, and a signal to have his ears checked by the veterinary surgeon.

NAIL CLIPPING

Your Lhasa Apso should be accustomed to having his nails trimmed at an early age, since it will be part of your maintenance routine throughout his life. Long nails can all too easily get caught in the Lhasa Apso's long coat,

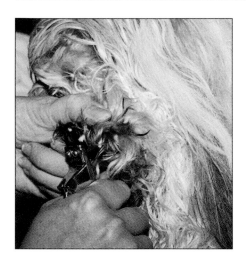

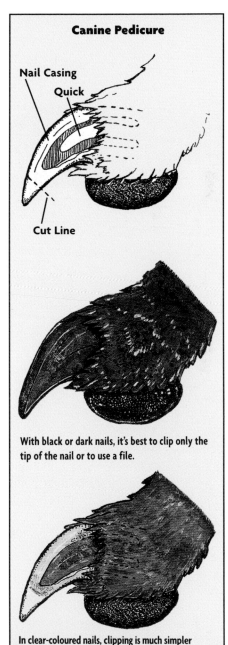

Canine Pedicure

Nail Casing

Quick

Cut Line

With black or dark nails, it's best to clip only the tip of the nail or to use a file.

In clear-coloured nails, clipping is much simpler because you can see the vein (or quick) that grows inside the casing.

Your Apso's nails should be trimmed regularly. When you can hear the nails clicking as the dog walks on a hard surface, the nails are too long. Pet shops sell special clippers for dog's nails.

and can be sharp if they scratch someone unintentionally. Also, a long nail has a better chance of ripping and bleeding, or causing the feet to spread. A good rule of thumb is that if you can hear your dog's nails clicking on the floor when he walks, his nails are too long.

Before you start cutting, make sure you can identify the 'quick' in each nail. The quick is a blood vessel that runs through the centre of each nail and grows rather close to the end. It will bleed if accidentally cut, which will be quite painful for the dog as it contains nerve endings. Keep some type of clotting agent on hand, such as a styptic pencil or styptic powder (the type used for shaving). This will stop the bleeding quickly when applied to the end of the cut nail. Do not panic if this happens, just stop the bleeding and talk soothingly

Clip only the bottom portion of the nail, avoiding the quick. If you cut into the quick, the nail will bleed and the dog will experience pain. A styptic pencil will stop the bleeding. Reassure the injured dog by talking quietly to him.

91

CAREFULLY clean around the Apso's eyes to remove tear stains.

to your dog. Once he has calmed down, move on to the next nail. It is better to clip a little at a time, particularly with black-nailed dogs.

Hold your pup steady as you begin trimming his nails; you do not want him to make any sudden movements or run away. Talk to him soothingly and stroke him as you clip. Holding his foot in your hand, simply take off the end of each nail in one quick clip. You can purchase nail clippers that are specially made for dogs; you can probably find them wherever you buy pet or grooming supplies.

Brush your Apso's teeth as often as possible; usually a weekly cleaning will suffice.

TRAVELLING WITH YOUR DOG
CAR TRAVEL
You should accustom your Lhasa Apso to riding in a car at an early age. You may or may not take him in the car often, but at

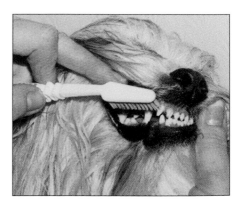

the very least he will need to go to the vet and you do not want these trips to be traumatic for the dog or a big hassle for you. The safest way for a dog to ride in the car is in his crate. If he uses a crate in the house, you can use the same crate for travel.

Put the pup in the crate and see how he reacts. If he seems uneasy, you can have a passenger hold him on his lap whilst you drive. Another option is a specially made safety harness for dogs, which straps the dog in much like a seat belt. Do not let the dog roam loose in the vehicle—this is very dangerous! If you should stop short, your dog can be thrown and injured. If the dog starts climbing on you and pestering you whilst you are driving, you will not be able to concentrate on the road. It is an unsafe situation for everyone—human and canine.

For long trips, be prepared to stop to let the dog relieve himself. Bring along whatever you need to clean up after him.

DID YOU KNOW?

If you are going on a long motor trip with your dog, be sure the hotels are dog friendly. Many hotels do not accept dogs. Also take along some ice that can be thawed and offered to your dog if he becomes overheated. Most dogs like to lick ice.

You should take along some paper kitchen towels and perhaps some old towelling for use should he have an accident in the car or suffer from travel sickness.

The most acceptable, safest way of travelling with your Lhasa Apso in a car is in a crate. It is dangerous for the dog to have free access to all parts of the vehicle whilst it is moving.

DID YOU KNOW?

Never leave your dog alone in the car. In hot weather your dog can die from the high temperature inside a closed vehicle; even a car parked in the shade can heat up very quickly. Leaving the window open is dangerous as well since the dog can hurt himself trying to get out.

AIR TRAVEL
Whilst it is possible to take a dog on a flight within Britain, this is fairly unusual and advance permission is always required. The dog will be required to travel in a fibreglass crate and you should always check in advance with the airline regarding specific requirements. To

help the dog be at ease, put one of his favourite toys in the crate with him. Do not feed the dog for at least six hours before the trip to minimise his need to relieve himself. However, certain regulations specify that water must always be made available to the dog in the crate.

Make sure your dog is properly identified and that your contact information appears on his ID tags and on his crate. Animals travel in a different area of the plane than human passengers so every rule must be strictly adhered to so as to prevent the risk of getting separated from your dog.

DID YOU KNOW?

When travelling, never let your dog off-lead in a strange area. Your dog could run away out of fear or decide to chase a passing chipmunk or cat or simply want to stretch his legs without restriction—you might never see your canine friend again.

DID YOU KNOW?

For international travel you will have to make arrangements well in advance (perhaps months), as countries' regulations pertaining to bringing in animals differ. There may be special health certificates and/or vaccinations that your dog will need before taking the trip, sometimes this has to be done within a certain time frame. In rabies-free countries, you will need to bring proof of the dog's rabies vaccination and there may be a quarantine period upon arrival.

BOARDING

So you want to take a family holiday—and you want to include all members of the family. You would probably make arrangements for accommodations ahead of time anyway, but this is especially important when travelling with a dog. You do not want to make an overnight stop at the only place around for miles and find out that they do not allow dogs. Also, you do not want to reserve a place for your family without confirming that you are travelling with a dog because if it is against their policy you may not have a place to stay.

Alternatively, if you are travelling and choose not to bring your Lhasa Apso, you will have to make arrangements for him whilst you are away. Some options are to take him to a neighbour's house to stay whilst

Should you find it necessary to board your Lhasa Apso whilst you are on holiday, locate a facility with clean accommodations and a friendly staff.

you are gone, to have a trusted neighbour stop by often or stay at your house, or bring your dog to a reputable boarding kennel. If you choose to board him at a kennel, you should visit in advance to see the facility, how clean they are and where the dogs are kept. Talk to some of the employees and see how they treat the dogs—have they experience in grooming long-coated dogs, do they spend time with the dogs, play with them, exercise them, etc.? Also find out the kennel's policy on vaccinations and what they require. This is for all of the dogs' safety, since when dogs are kept together, there is a greater risk of diseases being passed from dog to dog.

DID YOU KNOW?

If your dog gets lost, he is not able to ask for directions home.

Identification tags fastened to the collar give important information—the dog's name, the owner's name, the owner's address and a telephone number where the owner can be reached. This makes it easy for whoever finds the dog to contact the owner and arrange to have the dog returned. An added advantage is that a person will be more likely to approach a lost dog who has ID tags on his collar; it tells the person that this is somebody's pet rather than a stray. This is the easiest and fastest method of identification provided that the tags stay on the collar and the collar stays on the dog.

IDENTIFICATION

Your Lhasa Apso is your valued companion and friend. That is why you always keep a close eye on him and you have made sure that he cannot escape from the garden or wriggle out of his collar and run away from you. However, accidents can happen and there may come a time when your dog unexpectedly gets separated from you. If this unfortunate event should occur, the first thing on your mind will be finding him. Proper identification, including an ID tag, a tattoo, and possibly a microchip, will increase the chances of his being returned to you safely and quickly.

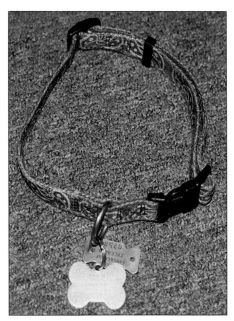

Your Lhasa Apso's ID tags should be securely attached to his collar.

Identification tags should be attached to your Apso's everyday collar. A dog in pet trim can wear his collar all the time; some owners prefer to remove the collars from dogs in full coat when the dogs are indoors.

Housebreaking and Training Your
LHASA APSO

Living with an untrained dog is a lot like owning a piano that you do not know how to play—it is a nice object to look at but it does not do much more than that to bring you pleasure. Now try taking piano lessons and suddenly the piano comes alive and brings forth magical sounds and rhythms that set your heart singing and your body swaying.

The same is true with your Lhasa Apso. Any dog is a big responsibility and, if not trained sensibly, may develop unacceptable behaviour that annoys you or even causes family friction.

To train your Lhasa Apso, you may like to enrol in an obedience class. Teach him good manners as you learn how and why he behaves the

way he does. Find out how to communicate with your dog and how to recognise and understand his communications with you. Suddenly the dog takes on a new role in your life—he is smart,

DID YOU KNOW?

If you start with a normal, healthy dog and give him time, patience and some carefully executed lessons, you will reap the rewards of that training for the life of the dog. And what a life it will be! The two of you will find immeasurable pleasure in the companionship you have built together with love, respect and understanding. Good luck and enjoy!

interesting, well behaved and fun to be with. He demonstrates his bond of devotion to you daily. In other words, your Lhasa Apso does wonders for your ego because he constantly reminds you that you are not only his leader, you are his hero!

Those involved with teaching dog obedience and counselling owners about their dogs' behaviour have discovered some interesting facts about dog ownership. For example, training dogs when they are puppies results in the highest rate of

DID YOU KNOW?

Taking your dog to an obedience school may be the best investment in time and money you can ever make. You will enjoy the benefits for the lifetime of your dog and you will have the opportunity to meet people with your similar expectations for companion dogs.

success in developing well-mannered and well-adjusted adult dogs. Training an older dog, from six months to six years of age, can produce almost equal results providing that the owner accepts the dog's slower rate of learning capability and is willing to work patiently to help the dog succeed at developing to his fullest potential. Unfortunately, many owners of untrained adult dogs lack the patience factor, so they do not persist until their dogs are successful at learning particular behaviours.

Training a puppy, aged 10 to 16 weeks (20 weeks at the most) is like working with a dry sponge in a pool of water. The pup soaks up whatever you show him and constantly looks for more things to do and learn. At this early age, his body is not yet producing hormones, and therein lies the reason for such a high rate of success. Without hormones, he is focused on his owners and not particularly interested in investigating other places, dogs, people, etc. You are his leader: his provider of food, water, shelter and security. He latches onto you and wants to stay close. He will usually follow you from room to room, will not let you out of his sight when you are outdoors with him, and respond in like manner to the people and animals you encounter. If you greet a friend warmly, he will be happy to greet the person as well. If, however, you are hesitant, even anxious, about the approach of a stranger, he will respond accordingly.

Once the puppy begins to produce hormones, his natural

You owe it to your puppy to train it in the basic principles of being a good citizen, including being housebroken and responding reliably to basic commands.

DID YOU KNOW?

Training a dog is a life experience. Many parents admit that much of what they know about raising children they learned from caring for their dogs. Dogs respond to love, fairness and guidance, just as children do. Become a good dog owner and you may become an even better parent.

DID YOU KNOW?

To a dog's way of thinking, your hands are like his mouth in terms of a defence mechanism. If you squeeze him too tightly, he might just bite you because that would be his normal response. This is not aggressive biting and, although all biting should be discouraged, you need the discipline in learning how to handle your dog.

There are usually classes within a reasonable distance from the owner's home, but you also do a lot to train your dog yourself. Sometimes there are classes available but the tuition is too costly. Whatever the circumstances, the solution to the problem of lack of lesson availability lies within the pages of this book.

This chapter is devoted to helping you train your Lhasa

curiosity emerges and he begins to investigate the world around him. It is at this time when you may notice that the untrained dog begins to wander away from you and even ignore your commands to stay close. When this behaviour becomes a problem, the owner has two choices: get rid of the dog or train him. It is strongly urged that you choose the latter option.

DID YOU KNOW?

Dogs are sensitive to their master's moods and emotions. Use your voice wisely when communicating with your dog. Never raise your voice at your dog unless you are angry and trying to correct him. 'Barking' at your dog can become as meaningless as 'dogspeak' is to you. Think before you bark!

Apso at home. If the recommended procedures are followed faithfully, you may expect positive results that will prove rewarding to both you and your dog.

Whether your new charge is a puppy or a mature adult, the methods of teaching and the techniques we use in training basic behaviours are the same. After all, no dog, whether puppy or adult, likes harsh or inhumane methods. All creatures, however,

DID YOU KNOW?

Mealtime should be a peaceful time for your puppy. Do not put his food and water bowls in a high-traffic area in the house. For example, give him his own little corner of the kitchen where he can eat undisturbed and where he will not be under foot. Do not allow small children or other family members to disrupt the pup when he is eating.

DID YOU KNOW?

The puppy should also have regular play and exercise sessions when he is with you or a family member. Exercise for a very young puppy can consist of a short walk around the house or garden. Playing can include fetching games with a large ball or a special raggy. (All puppies teethe and need soft things upon which to chew.) Remember to restrict play periods to indoors within his living area (the family room for example) until he is completely housetrained.

HOUSEBREAKING

You can train a puppy to relieve itself wherever you choose, but this must be somewhere suitable. You should bear in mind from the outset that when your puppy is old enough to go out in public places, any canine deposits must be removed at once. You will always have to carry with you a small plastic bag or 'poop-scoop.'

Outdoor training includes such surfaces as grass, dirt and cement. Indoor training usually means training your dog to newspaper.

When deciding on the surface and location that you will want your Lhasa Apso to use, be sure it is going to be permanent. Training your dog to grass and then

respond favourably to gentle motivational methods and sincere praise and encouragement. Now let us get started.

Male dogs lift their legs around the borders of the garden, but usually will not make puddle stains in the centre of your lawn.

DID YOU KNOW?

Your dog is actually training you at the same time you are training him. Dogs do things to get attention. They usually repeat whatever succeeds in getting your attention.

changing your mind two months later is extremely difficult for both dog and owner.

Next, choose the command you will use each and every time you want your puppy to void. 'Go hurry up' and 'Toilet' are examples of commands commonly used by dog owners.

Get in the habit of giving the puppy your chosen relief command before you take him out. That way, when he becomes an adult, you will be able to determine if he wants to go out when you ask him. A confirma-tion will be signs of interest, wagging his tail, watching you intently, going to the door, etc.

HOW MANY TIMES A DAY?

AGE	RELIEF TRIPS
To 14 weeks	10
14–22 weeks	8
22–32 weeks	6
Adulthood	4
(dog stops growing)	

These are estimates, of course, but they are a guide to the MINIMUM opportunities a dog should have each day to relieve itself.

PUPPY'S NEEDS
Puppy needs to relieve himself after play periods, after each meal, after he has been sleeping and any time he indicates that he is looking for a place to urinate or defecate.

The urinary and intestinal tract muscles of very young puppies are not fully developed. Therefore, like human babies, puppies need to relieve themselves frequently.

Take your puppy out often— every hour for an eight-week-old, for example, and always immedi-ately after sleeping and eating. The older the puppy, the less often he will need to relieve himself. Finally, as a mature healthy adult, he will require only three to five relief trips per day.

DID YOU KNOW?

Dogs will do anything for your attention. If you reward the dog when he is calm and resting, you will develop a well-mannered dog. If, on the other hand, you greet your dog excitedly and encourage him to wrestle and roughhouse with you, the dog will greet you the same way and you will have a hyper dog on your hands.

A well-trained Lhasa Apso is a wonderful combination of physical beauty and polite behaviour. Modhish Mumbo Jumbo Millie is co-owned by the author and Carol Ann Johnson.

HOUSING

Since the types of housing and control you provide for your puppy has a direct relationship on the success of housetraining, we consider the various aspects of both before we begin training.

Bringing a new puppy home and turning him loose in your house can be compared to turning a child loose in a sports arena and telling the child that the place is all his! The sheer enormity of the place would be too much for him to handle.

Instead, offer the puppy clearly defined areas where he can play, sleep, eat and live. A room of the house where the family

DID YOU KNOW?

Stand up straight and authoritatively when giving your dog commands. Do not issue commands when lying on the floor or lying on your back on the sofa. If you are on your hands and knees when you give a command, your dog will think you are positioning yourself to play.

DID YOU KNOW?

Dogs are the most honourable animals in existence. They consider another species (humans) as their own. They interface with you. You are their leader. Puppies perceive children to be on their level: their actions around small children are different than their behaviour around their adult masters.

gathers is the most obvious choice. Puppies are social animals and need to feel a part of the pack right from the start. Hearing your voice, watching you whilst you are doing things and smelling you nearby are all positive reinforcers that he is now a member of your pack. Usually a family room, the kitchen or a nearby adjoining breakfast area is ideal for providing safety and security for both puppy and owner.

Within that room there should be a smaller area which the puppy can call his own. An alcove, a wire or fibreglass dog crate or a fenced (not boarded!) corner from which he can view the activities of his new family will be fine. The size of the area or crate is the key factor here. The area must be large enough for the puppy to lie down

Your Apso should have a place to call its own that is both comfortable and conducive to housebreaking. A wire crate with bedding is all that is needed.

and stretch out as well as stand up without rubbing his head on the top, yet small enough so that he cannot relieve himself at one end and sleep at the other without coming into contact with his droppings until fully trained to relieve himself outside.

Dogs are, by nature, clean animals and will not remain close to their relief areas unless forced to do so. In those cases, they then become dirty dogs and usually remain that way for life.

Canine Development Schedule

It is important to understand how and at what age a puppy develops into adulthood. If you are a puppy owner, consult the following Canine Development Schedule to determine the stage of development your Lhasa Apso puppy is currently experiencing. This knowledge will help you as you work with the puppy in the weeks and months ahead.

Period	Age	Characteristics
FIRST TO THIRD	BIRTH TO SEVEN WEEKS	Puppy needs food, sleep and warmth, and responds to simple and gentle touching. Needs mother for security and disciplining. Needs littermates for learning and interacting with other dogs. Pup learns to function within a pack and learns pack order of dominance. Begin socialising with adults and children for short periods. Begins to become aware of its environment.
FOURTH	EIGHT TO TWELVE WEEKS	Brain is fully developed. Needs socialising with outside world. Remove from mother and littermates. Needs to change from canine pack to human pack. Human dominance necessary. Fear period occurs between 8 and 16 weeks. Avoid fright and pain.
FIFTH	THIRTEEN TO SIXTEEN WEEKS	Training and formal obedience should begin. Less association with other dogs, more with people, places, situations. Period will pass easily if you remember this is pup's change-to-adolescence time. Be firm and fair. Flight instinct prominent. Permissiveness and over-disciplining can do permanent damage. Praise for good behaviour.
JUVENILE	FOUR TO EIGHT MONTHS	Another fear period about 7 to 8 months of age. It passes quickly, but be cautious of fright and pain. Sexual maturity reached. Dominant traits established. Dog should understand sit, down, come and stay by now.

NOTE: THESE ARE APPROXIMATE TIME FRAMES. ALLOW FOR INDIVIDUAL DIFFERENCES IN PUPPIES.

The designated area should be lined with clean bedding and a toy. Water must always be available, in a non-spill container.

CONTROL

By control, we mean helping the puppy to create a lifestyle pattern that will be compatible to that of his human pack (YOU!). Just as we guide little children to learn our way of life, we must show the puppy when it is time to play, eat, sleep, exercise and even entertain himself.

Your puppy should always sleep in his crate. He should also learn that, during times of household confusion and excessive human activity such as at breakfast when family members are preparing for the day, he can

DID YOU KNOW?

Most of all, be consistent. Always take your dog to the same location, always use the same command, and always have him on lead when he is in his relief area, unless a fenced-in garden is available.

By following the Success Method, your puppy will be completely housetrained by the time his muscle and brain development reach maturity. Keep in mind that small breeds usually mature faster than large breeds, but all puppies should be trained by six months of age.

DID YOU KNOW?

By providing sleeping and resting quarters that fit the dog, and offering frequent opportunities to relieve himself outside his quarters, the puppy quickly learns that the outdoors (or the newspaper if you are training him to paper) is the place to go when he needs to urinate or defecate. It also reinforces his innate desire to keep his sleeping quarters clean. This, in turn, helps develop the muscle control that will eventually produce a dog with clean living habits.

play by himself in relative safety and comfort in his designated area. Each time you leave the puppy alone, he should understand exactly where he is to stay. Puppies are chewers. They cannot tell the difference between lamp cords, television wires, shoes, table legs, etc. Chewing into a television wire, for example, can be fatal to the puppy whilst a shorted wire can start a fire in the house.

If the puppy chews on the arm of the chair when he is alone, you will probably discipline him angrily when you get home. Thus, he makes the association that your coming home means he is going to be punished. (He will not remember chewing up the chair and is incapable of making the association of the discipline with

DID YOU KNOW?

If you want to be successful in training your dog, you have four rules to obey yourself:
1. Develop an understanding of how a dog thinks.
2. Do not blame the dog for lack of communication.
3. Define your dog's personality and act accordingly.
4. Have patience and be consistent.

his naughty deed.)

Other times of excitement, such as family parties, etc., can be fun for the puppy providing he can view the activities from the security of his designated area. He is not underfoot and he is not being fed all sorts of titbits that will probably cause him stomach distress, yet he still feels a part of the fun.

SCHEDULE

A puppy should be taken to his relief area each time he is released from his designated area, after meals, after a play session, when he first awakens in the morning (at age eight weeks, this can mean 5 a.m.!). The puppy will indicate

THE SUCCESS METHOD
6 Steps to Successful Crate Training

1 Tell the puppy 'Crate time!' and place him in the crate with a small treat (a piece of cheese or half of a biscuit). Let him stay in the crate for five minutes while you are in the same room. Then release him and praise lavishly. Never release him when he is fussing. Wait until he is quiet before you let him out.

2 Repeat Step 1 several times a day.

3 The next day, place the puppy in the crate as before. Let him stay there for ten minutes. Do this several times.

4 Continue building time in five-minute increments until the puppy stays in his crate for 30 minutes with you in the room. Always take him to his relief area after prolonged periods in his crate.

5 Now go back to Step 1 and let the puppy stay in his crate for five minutes, this time while you are out of the room.

6 Once again, build crate time in five-minute increments with you out of the room. When the puppy will stay willingly in his crate (he may even fall asleep!) for 30 minutes with you out of the room, he will be ready to stay in it for several hours at a time.

that he's ready 'to go' by circling or sniffing busily—do not misinterpret these signs. For a puppy less than ten weeks of age, a routine of taking him out every hour is necessary. As the puppy grows, he will be able to wait for longer periods of time.

Keep trips to his relief area short. Stay no more than five or six minutes and then return to the house. If he goes during that time, praise him lavishly and take him indoors immediately. If he does not, but he has an accident when you go back indoors, pick him up

Always clean up after your dog, even if it is in your own garden.

immediately, say 'No! No!' and return to his relief area. Wait a few minutes, then return to the house again. never hit a puppy or rub his face in urine or excrement when he has an accident!

Once indoors, put the puppy in his crate until you have had time to clean up his accident. Then release him to the family area and watch him more closely than before. Chances are, his accident was a result of your not

DID YOU KNOW?

Do not carry your dog to his toilet area. Lead him there on a leash or, better yet, encourage him to follow you to the spot. If you start carrying him to his spot, you might end up doing this routine forever and your dog will have the satisfaction of having trained YOU.

picking up his signal or waiting too long before offering him the opportunity to relieve himself. Never hold a grudge against the puppy for accidents.

Let the puppy learn that going outdoors means it is time to relieve himself, not play. Once trained, he will be able to play indoors and out and still differentiate between the times for play versus the times for relief.

Help him develop regular hours for naps, being alone, playing by himself and just resting, all in his crate. Encourage him to entertain himself whilst you are busy with your activities. Let him learn that having you near is comforting, but it is not your main purpose in life to provide him with undivided attention.

Each time you put a puppy in his own area, use the same command, whatever suits best. Soon, he will run to his crate or special area when he hears you say those words.

Crate training provides safety for you, the puppy and the home. It also provides the puppy with a feeling of security, and that helps the puppy achieve self-confidence and clean habits.

Remember that one of the primary ingredients in housetraining your puppy is control. Regardless of your lifestyle, there will always be occasions when you will need to have a place where your dog can stay and be happy and safe. Training is the answer for now and in the future.

In conclusion, a few key elements are really all you need for a successful house training method—consistency, frequency, praise, control and supervision. By following these procedures with a normal, healthy puppy, you and the puppy will soon be past the stage of 'accidents' and ready to move on to a full and rewarding life together.

ROLES OF DISCIPLINE, REWARD AND PUNISHMENT

Discipline, training one to act in accordance with rules, brings order to life. It is as simple as that. Without discipline, particularly in a group society, chaos reigns supreme and the group will eventually perish. Humans and canines are social animals and need some form of discipline in order to function effectively. They must procure food, protect their home base and their young and reproduce to keep the species going.

If there were no discipline in the lives of social animals, they would eventually die from starvation and/or predation by other stronger animals.

In the case of domestic canines, dogs need discipline in their lives in order to understand how their pack (you and other family members) functions and how they must act in order to survive.

A large humane society in a highly populated area recently surveyed dog owners regarding their satisfaction with their relationships with their dogs. People who had trained their dogs were 75% more satisfied with their pets than those who had never trained their dogs.

DID YOU KNOW?

Success that comes by luck is usually short lived. Success that comes by well-thought-out proven methods is often more easily achieved and permanent. This is the Success Method. It is designed to give you, the puppy owner, a simple yet proven way to help your puppy develop clean living habits and a feeling of security in his new environment.

Dr Edward Thorndike, a psychologist, established *Thorndike's Theory of Learning*, which states that a behaviour that results in a pleasant event tends to be repeated. A behaviour that results in an unpleasant event tends not to be repeated. It is this theory on which training methods are based today. For example, if you manipulate a dog to perform a specific behaviour and reward him for doing it, he is likely to do it again because he enjoyed the end result.

Occasionally, punishment, a penalty inflicted for an offence, is necessary. The best type of punishment often comes from an outside source. For example, a child is

DID YOU KNOW?

Practice Makes Perfect!
• Have training lessons with your dog every day in several short segments—three to five times a day for a few minutes at a time is ideal.
• Do not have long practice sessions. The dog will become easily bored.
• Never practice when you are tired, ill, worried or in an otherwise negative mood. This will transmit to the dog and may have an adverse effect on its performance.

Think fun, short and above all POSITIVE! End each session on a high note, rather than a failed exercise, and make sure to give a lot of praise. Enjoy the training and help your dog enjoy it, too.

DID YOU KNOW?

Never train your dog, puppy or adult, when you are mad or in a sour mood. Dogs are very sensitive to human feelings, especially anger, and if your dog senses that you are angry or upset, he will connect your anger with his training and learn to resent or fear his training sessions.

told not to touch the stove because he may get burned. He disobeys and touches the stove. In doing so, he receives a burn. From that time on, he respects the heat of the stove and avoids contact with it. Therefore, a behaviour that results in an unpleasant event tends not to be repeated.

A good example of a dog learning the hard way is the dog who chases the house cat. He is told many times to leave the cat alone, yet he persists in teasing the cat. Then, one day he begins chasing the cat but the cat turns and swipes a claw across the dog's face, leaving him with a painful gash on his nose. The final result is that the dog stops chasing the cat.

TRAINING EQUIPMENT
COLLAR AND LEAD
For a Lhasa Apso the collar and lead that you use for training must be one with which you are easily able to work, not too heavy for the dog and perfectly safe.

TRAINING BEGINS: ASK THE DOG A QUESTION

In order to teach your dog anything, you must first get his attention. After all, he cannot learn anything if he is looking away from you with his mind on something else.

To get his attention, ask him, 'School?' and immediately walk over to him and give him a treat as you tell him 'Good dog.' Wait a minute or two and repeat the routine, this time with a treat in your hand as you approach within a foot of the dog. Do not go directly to him, but stop about a foot short of him and hold out the treat as you ask, 'School?' He will see you approaching with a treat in your hand and most likely begin walking toward you. As you meet, give him the treat and praise again.

Dogs are easily motivated in training by food rewards. Use treats sparingly since you must eventually wean the dog away from them.

TREATS

Have a bag of treats on hand. Something nutritious and easy to swallow works best. Use a soft treat, a chunk of cheese or a piece of cooked chicken rather than a dry biscuit. By the time the dog gets done chewing a dry treat, he will forget why he is being rewarded in the first place! Using food rewards will not teach a dog to beg at the table— the only way to teach a dog to beg at the table is to give him food from the table. In training, rewarding the dog with a food treat will help him associate praise and the treats with learning new behaviours that obviously please his owner.

DID YOU KNOW?

Dogs do not understand our language. They can be trained to react to a certain sound, at a certain volume. If you say 'No, Oliver' in a very soft pleasant voice it will not have the same meaning as 'No, Oliver!!' when you shout it as loud as you can. You should never use the dog's name during a reprimand, just the command NO!! Since dogs don't understand words, comics use dogs trained with opposite meanings. Thus, when the comic commands his dog to SIT the dog will stand up; and vice versa.

111

The third time, ask the question, have a treat in your hand and walk only a short distance toward the dog so that he must walk almost all the way to you. As he reaches you, give him the treat and praise again.

Don't overdo it with food rewards—a puppy or small dog has a relatively low daily calorie requirement and small treats can add up quickly.

By this time, the dog will probably be getting the idea that if he pays attention to you, especially when you ask that question, it will pay off in treats and fun activities for him. In other words, he learns that 'school' means doing fun things with you that result in treats and positive attention for him.

Remember that the dog does not understand your verbal language, he only recognises sounds. Your question translates to a series of sounds for him, and those sounds become the signal to go to you and pay attention; if he does, he will get to interact with you plus receive treats and praise.

THE BASIC COMMANDS
TEACHING SIT

Now that you have the dog's attention, attach his lead and hold it in your left hand and a food treat in your right. Place your food hand at the dog's nose and let him lick the treat but not take it from you. Say 'Sit' and slowly raise your food hand from in front of the dog's nose up over his head so that he is looking at the ceiling. As he bends his head upward, he will have to bend his knees to maintain his balance. As he bends his knees, he will assume a sit position. At that point, release the food treat and praise lavishly with comments such as 'Good dog! Good sit!', etc. Remember to always praise enthusiastically, because dogs relish verbal praise from their owners and feel so proud of themselves whenever they accomplish a behaviour.

DID YOU KNOW?

Dogs are as different from each other as people are. What works for one dog may not work for another. Have an open mind. If one method of training is unsuccessful, try another.

You will not use food forever in getting the dog to obey your commands. Food is only used to teach new behaviours, and once the dog knows what you want when you give a specific command, you will wean him off of the food treats but still maintain the verbal praise. After all, you will always have your voice with you, and there will be many times when you have no food rewards but expect the dog to obey.

Teaching basic commands can be done with a combination of verbal directions and hand signals.

TEACHING DOWN

Teaching the down exercise is easy when you understand how the dog perceives the down position, and it is very difficult when you do not. Dogs perceive the down position as a submissive one, therefore teaching the down exercise using a forceful method can sometimes make the dog develop such a fear of the down that he either runs away when you say 'Down' or he attempts to snap at the person who tries to force him down.

Have the dog sit close alongside your left leg, facing in the same direction as you are. Hold the lead in your left hand and a food treat in your right.

Now place your left hand lightly on the top of the dog's shoulders where they meet above the spinal cord. Do not push down on the dog's shoulders; simply rest your left hand there so you can

DID YOU KNOW?

A dog in jeopardy never lies down. He stays alert on his feet because instinct tells him that he may have to run away or fight for his survival. Therefore, if a dog feels threatened or anxious, he will not lie down. Consequently, it is important to have the dog calm and relaxed as he learns the down exercise.

Start teaching the stay by standing very close to the dog. When he is successful with this, start to move away from him gradually and have him stay for longer periods of time.

guide the dog to lie down close to your left leg rather than to swing away from your side when he drops.

Now place the food hand at the dog's nose, say 'Down' very softly (almost a whisper), and slowly lower the food hand to the dog's front feet. When the food hand reaches the floor, begin moving it forward along the floor in front of the dog. Keep talking softly to the dog, saying things like, 'Do you want this treat? You can do this, good dog.' Your reassuring tone of voice will help calm the dog as he tries to follow the food hand in order to get the treat.

When the dog's elbows touch the floor, release the food and praise softly. Try to get the dog to maintain that down position for several seconds before you let him sit up again. The goal here is to get

the dog to settle down and not feel threatened in the down position.

TEACHING STAY

It is easy to teach the dog to stay in either a sit or a down position. Again, we use food and praise during the teaching process as we help the dog to understand exactly what it is that we are expecting him to do.

To teach the sit/stay, start with the dog sitting on your left side as before and hold the lead in your left hand. Have a food treat in your right hand and place your food hand at the dog's nose. Say 'Stay' and step out on your right foot to stand directly in front of the dog, toe to toe, as he licks and nibbles the treat. Be sure to keep his head facing upward to maintain the sit position. Count to five and then swing around to stand next to the dog again with him on your left. As soon as you get back to the original position, release the food and praise lavishly.

To teach the down/stay, do the down as previously described. As soon as the dog lies down, say 'Stay' and step out on your right foot just as you did in the sit/stay. Count to five and then return to stand beside the dog with him on your left side. Release the treat and praise as always.

Within a week or ten days, you can begin to add a bit of distance between you and your dog when you leave him. When you do, use your left hand open with the palm facing the dog as a stay signal, much the same as the hand signal a police officer uses to stop traffic at an intersection. Hold the food treat in your right hand as before, but this time the food is not touching the dog's nose. He will watch the food hand and quickly learn that he is going to get that treat as soon as you return to his side.

When you can stand 1 metre away from your dog for 30 seconds, you can then begin building time and distance in both stays. Eventually, the dog can be expected to remain in the stay position for prolonged periods of time until you return to him or call him to you. Always praise lavishly when he stays.

TEACHING COME

If you make teaching 'come' a fun experience, you should never have a 'student' that does not love the game or that fails to come when called. The secret, it seems, is never to teach the word 'come.'

At times when an owner most wants his dog to come when called, the owner is likely upset or anxious and he allows these feelings to come through in the tone of his voice when he calls his dog. Hearing that desperation in his owner's voice, the dog fears the results of going to him and therefore either disobeys outright or runs in the opposite direction. The secret, therefore, is to teach the dog a game and, when you want him to come to you, simply play the game. It is practically a no-fail solution!

To begin, have several members of your family take a few food treats and each go into a different room in the house. Take turns calling the dog, and each person should celebrate the dog's finding him with a treat and lots of happy praise. When a person calls the dog, he is actually inviting the dog to find him and get a treat as a reward for 'winning.'

A few turns of the 'Where are you?' game and the dog will figure out that everyone is playing the game and that each person has a big celebration awaiting his success at locating them. Once he learns to love the game, simply calling out 'Where are you?' will bring him running from wherever he is when he hears that all-important question.

The come command is recognised as one of the most important things to teach a dog, but there are trainers who work with thousands of dogs and never teach the actual word 'Come.' Yet these dogs will race to respond to a person who uses the dog's name followed by 'Where are you?' For example, a woman has a 12-year-old companion dog who went blind, but who never fails to locate her owner when asked, 'Where are you?'

Children particularly love to play this game with their dogs. Children can hide in smaller places like a shower or bathtub, behind a bed or under a table. The dog needs to work a little bit harder to find these hiding places, but when he does he loves to celebrate with a treat and a tussle with a favourite youngster.

TEACHING HEEL

Heeling means that the dog walks beside the owner without pulling. It takes time and patience on the owner's part to succeed at teaching the dog that he (the owner) will not proceed unless the dog is walking calmly beside him. Pulling out ahead on the lead is definitely not acceptable.

Begin with holding the lead in your left hand as the dog sits beside your left leg. Move the loop end of the lead to your right hand but keep your left hand

DID YOU KNOW?

When calling the dog, do not say 'Come.' Say things like, 'Rover, where are you? See if you can find me! I have a cookie for you!' Keep up a constant line of chatter with coaxing sounds and frequent questions such as, 'Where are you?' The dog will learn to follow the sound of your voice to locate you and receive his reward.

short on the lead so it keeps the dog in close next to you.

Say 'Heel' and step forward on your left foot. Keep the dog close to you and take three steps. Stop and have the dog sit next to you in what we now call the 'heel position.' Praise verbally, but do not touch the dog. Hesitate a moment and begin again with 'Heel,' taking three steps and stopping, at which point the dog is told to sit again.

Your goal here is to have the dog walk those three steps without pulling on the lead. When he will walk calmly beside you for three steps without pulling, increase the number of steps you take to five. When he will walk politely beside you whilst you take five steps, you can increase the length of your walk to ten steps. Keep increasing the length of your stroll until the dog will walk quietly beside you without pulling as long as you want him to heel. When you stop heeling, indicate to the dog that the exercise is over by verbally praising as you pet him and say 'OK, good dog.' The 'OK' is used as a release word meaning that the exercise is finished and the dog is free to relax.

If you are dealing with a dog who insists on pulling you around, simply 'put on your brakes' and stand your ground until the dog realises that the two of you are not going anywhere

Heeling is not just for show dogs. All dogs must be trained to heel so that they will walk politely during everyday walks.

until he is beside you and moving at your pace, not his. It may take some time just standing there to convince the dog that you are the leader and you will be the one to decide on the direction and speed of your travel.

DID YOU KNOW?

If you begin teaching the heel by taking long walks and letting the dog pull you along, he misinterprets this action as an acceptable form of taking a walk. When you pull back on the lead to counteract his pulling, he reads that tug as a signal to pull even harder!

117

Each time the dog looks up at you or slows down to give a slack lead between the two of you, quietly praise him and say, 'Good heel. Good dog.' Eventually, the dog will begin to respond and within a few days he will be walking politely beside you without pulling on the lead. At first, the training sessions should be kept short and very positive; soon the dog will be able to walk nicely with you for increasingly longer distances. Remember also to give the dog free time and the opportunity to run and play when you are done with heel practice.

WEANING OFF FOOD IN TRAINING

Food is used in training new behaviours. Once the dog understands what behaviour goes with a specific command, it is time to start weaning him off the food treats. At first, give a treat after each exercise. Then, start to give a treat only after every other exercise. Mix up the times when you offer a food reward and the times when you only offer praise so that the dog will never know when he is going to receive both food and praise and when he is going to receive only praise. This is called a variable ratio reward system and it proves successful because there is always the chance that the owner will produce a treat, so the dog never stops trying for that reward. No matter what, ALWAYS give verbal praise.

OBEDIENCE CLASSES

It is a good idea to enrol in an obedience class if one is available in your area. If yours is a show dog, ringcraft classes would be more appropriate.. Many areas have dog clubs that offer basic obedience training as well as preparatory classes for obedience competition. There are also local dog trainers who offer similar classes.

At obedience trials, dogs can earn titles at various levels of competition. The beginning levels of competition include basic

DID YOU KNOW?

Occasionally, a dog and owner who have not attended formal classes have been able to earn entry-level titles by obtaining competition rules and regulations from a local kennel club and practising on their own to a degree of perfection. Obtaining the higher level titles, however, almost always requires extensive training under the tutelage of experienced instructors. In addition, the more difficult levels require more specialised equipment whereas the lower levels do not.

behaviours such as sit, down, heel, etc. The more advanced levels of competition include jumping, retrieving, scent discrimination and signal work. The advanced levels require a dog and owner to put a lot of time and effort into their training and the titles that can be earned at these levels of competition are very prestigious.

OTHER ACTIVITIES FOR LIFE
Whether a dog is trained in the structured environment of a class or alone with his owner at home, there are many activities that can bring fun and rewards to both owner and dog once they have mastered basic control.

DID YOU KNOW?

A basic obedience beginner's class usually lasts for six to eight weeks. Dog and owner attend an hour-long lesson once a week and practice for a few minutes, several times a day, each day at home. If done properly, the whole procedure will result in a well-mannered dog and an owner who delights in living with a pet that is eager to please and enjoys doing things with his owner.

Teaching the dog to help out around the home, in the garden or on the farm provides great satisfaction to both dog and owner. In addition, the dog's help makes life a little easier for his owner and raises his stature as a valued companion to his family. It helps give the dog a purpose by occupying his mind and providing an outlet for his energy.

Hiking is an exciting and healthy activity that the dog can be taught without assistance from more than his owner. The exercise of walking and climbing is good for man and dog alike, and the bond that they develop together is priceless.

If you are interested in participating in organised competition with your Lhasa Apso, there are activities other than obedience in which you and your dog can become involved. Agility is a popular and fun sport where dogs run through an obstacle course that includes various jumps, tunnels and other exercises to test the dog's speed and coordination. The owners run through the course beside their dogs to give commands and to guide them through the course. Although competitive, the focus is on fun—it's fun to do, fun to watch, and great exercise.

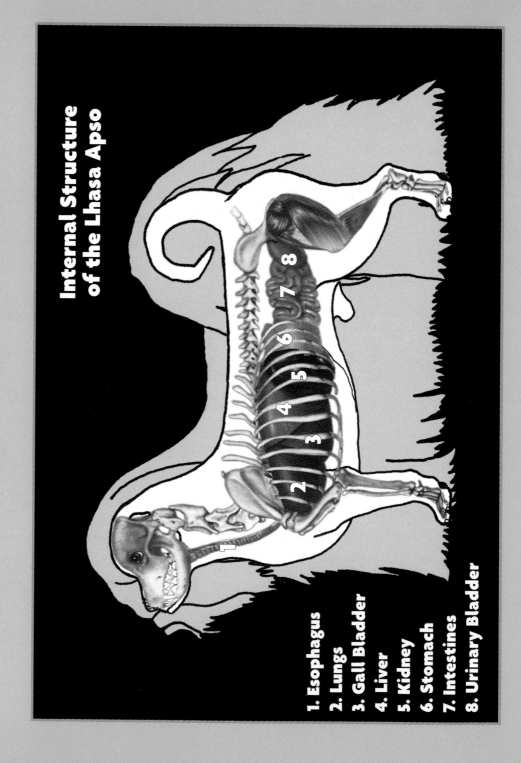

Internal Structure of the Lhasa Apso

1. Esophagus
2. Lungs
3. Gall Bladder
4. Liver
5. Kidney
6. Stomach
7. Intestines
8. Urinary Bladder

Dogs suffer many of the same physical illnesses as people. They might even share many of the same psychological problems. Since people usually know more about human diseases than canine maladies, many of the terms used in this chapter will be familiar but not necessarily those used by veterinary surgeons. We will use the term x-ray, instead of the more acceptable term radiograph. We will also use the familiar term symptoms even though dogs don't have symptoms, which are verbal descriptions of the patient's feelings: dogs have clinical signs. Since dogs can't speak, we have to look for clinical signs...but we still use the term symptoms in this book.

As a general rule, medicine is practised. That term is not arbitrary. Medicine is a constantly changing art as we learn more and more about genetics, electronic aids (like CAT scans) and daily laboratory advances. There are many dog maladies, like canine hip dysplasia, which are not universally treated in the same manner. Some veterinary surgeons opt for surgery more often than others do.

SELECTING A VETERINARY SURGEON
Your selection of a veterinary surgeon should not be based upon personality (as most are) but upon their convenience to your home. You want a doctor who is close because you might have emergencies or need to make multiple visits for treatments. You want a doctor who has services

that you might require such as a boarding kennel and grooming facilities, as well as sophisticated pet supplies and a good reputation for ability and responsiveness. There is nothing more frustrating than having to

Before you buy your Lhasa Apso, meet and interview the veterinary surgeons in your area. Take everything into consideration; discuss his background, specialities, fees, emergency policy, etc.

A typical American vet's income categorised according to services performed. This survey dealt with small-animal (pets) practices.

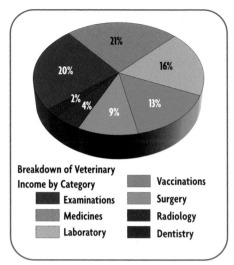

Breakdown of Veterinary Income by Category

- Examinations
- Medicines
- Laboratory
- Vaccinations
- Surgery
- Radiology
- Dentistry

wait a day or more to get a response from your veterinary surgeon.

All veterinary surgeons are licensed and their diplomas and/or certificates should be displayed in their waiting rooms. There are, however, many veterinary specialties that usually require further studies and internships. There are specialists in heart problems (veterinary cardiologists), skin problems (veterinary dermatologists), teeth and gum problems (veterinary dentists), eye problems (veterinary ophthalmologists), X-rays (veterinary radiologists), and surgeons who have specialities in bones, muscles or other organs. Most veterinary surgeons do routine surgery such as neutering, stitching up wounds and

docking tails for those breeds in which such is required for show purposes. When the problem affecting your dog is serious, it is not unusual or impudent to get another medical opinion, although in Britain you are obliged to advise the vets concerned about this. You might also want to compare costs amongst several veterinary surgeons. Sophisticated health care and veterinary services can be very costly. Don't be bashful about discussing these costs with your veterinary surgeon or his (her) staff. It is not infrequent that important decisions are based upon financial considerations.

PREVENTATIVE MEDICINE
It is much easier, less costly and more effective to practise preventative medicine than to fight bouts of illness and disease. Properly bred puppies come from parents that were selected based upon their genetic disease profile. Their mothers should have been vaccinated, free of all internal and external parasites, and properly nourished. For these reasons, a visit to the veterinary surgeon who cared for the dam (mother) is recommended. The dam can pass on disease resistance to her puppies, which can last for eight to ten weeks. She can also pass on parasites

First Aid at a Glance

Burns
Place the affected area under cool water; use ice if only a small area is burnt.

Car accident
Move dog from roadway with blanket; seek veterinary aid.

Bee/Insect bites
Apply ice to relieve swelling; antihistamine dosed properly.

Shock
Calm the dog, keep him warm; seek immediate veterinary help.

Animal bites
Clean any bleeding area; apply pressure until bleeding subsides; go to the vet.

Nosebleed
Apply cold compress to the nose; apply pressure to any visible abrasion.

Spider bites
Use cold compress and a pressurised pack to inhibit venom's spreading.

Bleeding
Apply pressure above the area; treat wound by applying a cotton pack.

Antifreeze poisoning
Immediately induce vomiting by using hydrogen peroxide.

Heat stroke
Submerge dog in cold bath; cool down with fresh air and water; go to the vet.

Fish hooks
Removal best handled by vet; hook must be cut in order to remove.

Frostbite/Hypothermia
Warm the dog with a warm bath, electric blankets or hot water bottles.

Snake bites
Pack ice around bite; contact vet quickly; identify snake for proper antivenin.

Abrasions
Clean the wound and wash out thoroughly with fresh water; apply antiseptic.

 Remember: an injured dog may attempt to bite a helping hand from fear and confusion. Always muzzle the dog before trying to offer assistance.

and many infections. That's why you should visit the veterinary surgeon who cared for the dam.

WEANING TO FIVE MONTHS OLD

Puppies should be weaned by the time they are about two months old. A puppy that remains for at least eight weeks with its mother and litter mates usually adapts better to other dogs and people later in its life.

Some new owners have their puppy examined by a veterinary surgeon immediately, which is a good idea. Vaccination programmes usually begin when the puppy is very young.

The puppy will have its teeth examined and have its skeletal conformation and general health checked prior to certification by the veterinary surgeon. Puppies in certain breeds have problems with their kneecaps, eye cataracts and other eye problems, heart murmurs and

DID YOU KNOW?

Male dogs are neutered. The operation removes the testicles and requires that the dog be anaesthetised. Recovery takes about one week. Females are spayed. This is major surgery and it usually takes a bitch two weeks to recover.

undescended testicles. They may also have personality problems and your veterinary surgeon might have training in temperament evaluation.

VACCINATION SCHEDULING

Most vaccinations are given by injection and should only be done by a veterinary surgeon. Both he and you should keep a record of the date of the injection, the identification of the vaccine and the amount given. Some vets give a first vaccination at eight weeks, but most dog breeders prefer the course not to commence until about ten weeks because of negating any antibodies passed on by the dam. The vaccination scheduling is usually based on a 15-day cycle. You must take your vet's advice as to when to vaccinate as this may differ according to the vaccine used. Most vaccinations immunise your puppy against viruses.

The usual vaccines contain immunising doses of several

DID YOU KNOW?

Caring for the puppy starts before the puppy is born by keeping the dam healthy and well-nourished. Most puppies have worms, even if they are not evident, so a worming programme is essential. The worms continually shed eggs except during their dormant stage, when they just rest in the tissues of the puppy. During this stage they are not evident during a routine examination.

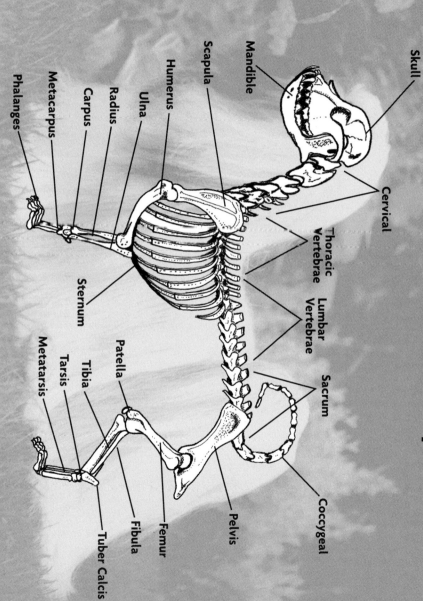

Normal Lhasa Apso Skeleton

Skull

Mandible

Cervical

Thoracic Vertebrae

Lumbar Vertebrae

Sacrum

Coccygeal

Scapula

Humerus

Ulna

Radius

Carpus

Metacarpus

Phalanges

Sternum

Pelvis

Patella

Femur

Fibula

Tibia

Tarsis

Metatarsis

Tuber Calcis

HEALTH AND VACCINATION SCHEDULE

AGE IN WEEKS:	3RD	6TH	8TH	10TH	12TH	14TH	16TH	20-24TH
Worm Control	✔	✔	✔	✔	✔	✔	✔	✔
Neutering								✔
Heartworm*		✔						✔
Parvovirus		✔		✔		✔		✔
Distemper			✔		✔		✔	
Hepatitis			✔		✔		✔	
Leptospirosis		✔		✔		✔		
Parainfluenza		✔		✔		✔		
Dental Examination			✔					✔
Complete Physical			✔					✔
Temperament Testing			✔					
Coronavirus					✔			
Kennel Cough		✔						
Hip Dysplasia							✔	
Rabies*								✔

Vaccinations are not instantly effective. It takes about two weeks for the dog's immunisation system to develop antibodies. Most vaccinations require annual booster shots. Your veterinary surgeon should guide you in this regard.
*Not applicable in the United Kingdom

different viruses such as distemper, parvovirus, parainfluenza and hepatitis. There are other vaccines available when the puppy is at risk. You should rely

DID YOU KNOW?

Not every dog's ears are the same. Ears that are open to the air are healthier than ears with poor air circulation. Sometimes a dog can have two differently shaped ears. You should not probe inside your dog's ears. Only clean that which is accessible with a wad of soft cotton wool.

upon professional advice. This is especially true for the booster-shot programme. Most vaccination programmes require a booster when the puppy is a year old and once a year thereafter. In some cases, circumstances may require more frequent immunisations. Kennel cough, more formally known as tracheobronchitis, is treated with a vaccine that is sprayed into the dog's nostrils. Kennel cough is usually included in routine vaccination, but this is often not so effective as for other major diseases.

FIVE MONTHS TO ONE YEAR OF AGE
Unless you intend to breed or show your dog, neutering the puppy at six months of age is recommended. Discuss this with your veterinary surgeon.

By the time your Lhasa Apso is seven or eight months of age, he can be seriously evaluated for his conformation to the standard, thus determining show potential and desirability as a sire or dam. If the puppy is not top class and therefore is not a candidate for a serious breeding programme, most professionals advise neutering the puppy. Neutering has proven to be extremely beneficial to both

male and female puppies. Besides eliminating the possibility of pregnancy, it inhibits (but does not prevent) breast cancer in bitches and prostate cancer in

DID YOU KNOW?

Vaccines do not work all the time. Sometimes dogs are allergic to them and many times the antibodies, which are supposed to be stimulated by the vaccine, just are not produced. You should keep your dog in the veterinary clinic for an hour after it is vaccinated to be sure there are no allergic reactions.

Disease	What is it?	What causes it?	Symptoms
Leptospirosis	Severe disease that affects the internal organs; can be spread to people.	A bacterium, which is often carried by rodents, that enters through mucous membranes and spreads quickly throughout the body.	Range from fever, vomiting and loss of appetite in less severe cases to shock, irreversible kidney damage and possibly death in most severe cases.
Rabies	Potentially deadly virus that infects warm-blooded mammals. Not seen in United Kingdom.	Bite from a carrier of the virus, mainly wild animals.	1st stage: dog exhibits change in behaviour, fear. 2nd stage: dog's behaviour becomes more aggressive. 3rd stage: loss of coordination, trouble with bodily functions.
Parvovirus	Highly contagious virus, potentially deadly.	Ingestion of the virus, which is usually spread through the faeces of infected dogs.	Most common: severe diarrhoea. Also vomiting, fatigue, lack of appetite.
Kennel cough	Contagious respiratory infection.	Combination of types of bacteria and virus. Most common: *Bordetella bronchiseptica* bacteria and parainfluenza virus.	Chronic cough.
Distemper	Disease primarily affecting respiratory and nervous system.	Virus that is related to the human measles virus.	Mild symptoms such as fever, lack of appetite and mucous secretion progress to evidence of brain damage, 'hard pad.'
Hepatitis	Virus primarily affecting the liver.	Canine adenovirus type I (CAV-1). Enters system when dog breathes in particles.	Lesser symptoms include listlessness, diarrhoea, vomiting. More severe symptoms include 'blue-eye' (clumps of virus in eye).
Coronavirus	Virus resulting in digestive problems.	Virus is spread through infected dog's faeces.	Stomach upset evidenced by lack of appetite, vomiting, diarrhoea

male dogs. Under no circumstances should a bitch be spayed prior to her first season.

DOGS OLDER THAN ONE YEAR

Continue to visit the veterinary surgeon at least once a year. There is no such disease as old age, but bodily functions do change with age. The eyes and ears are no longer as efficient. Liver, kidney and intestinal functions often decline. Proper dietary changes, recommended by your veterinary surgeon, can make life more pleasant for the ageing Lhasa Apso and you.

SKIN PROBLEMS IN LHASA APSOS

Veterinary surgeons are consulted by dog owners for skin problems more than any other group of diseases or maladies. Dogs' skin is almost as sensitive as human skin and both suffer almost the same ailments. (Though the occurrence of acne in dogs is rare!) For this reason, veterinary dermatology has developed into a speciality practised by many veterinary surgeons.

Since many skin problems have visual symptoms that are almost identical, it requires the skill of an experienced veterinary dermatologist to identify and cure many of the more severe skin disorders. Pet shops sell many treatments for skin

DID YOU KNOW?

A dental examination is in order when the dog is between six months and one year of age so any permanent teeth that have erupted incorrectly can be corrected. It is important to begin a brushing routine, preferably using a two-sided brushing technique, whereby both sides of the tooth are brushed at the same time. Durable nylon and safe edible chews should be a part of your puppy's arsenal for good health, good teeth and pleasant breath. The vast majority of dogs three to four years old and older has diseases of their gums from lack of dental attention. Using the various types of dental chews can be very effective in controlling dental plaque.

problems but most of the treatments are directed at symptoms and not the underlying problem(s). If your dog is suffering from a skin disorder, you should seek professional assistance as quickly as possible. As with all diseases, the earlier a problem is identified and treated, the more successful is the cure.

INHERITED SKIN PROBLEMS

Many skin disorders are inherited and some are fatal. For example, Acrodermatitis is an inherited disease that is transmitted by both parents. The parents, who appear (phenotypically) normal, have a recessive gene for acrodermatitis, meaning that they carry, but are not affected by the disease.

Acrodermatitis is just one example of how difficult it is to prevent congenital dog diseases. The cost and skills required to ascertain whether two dogs should be mated are too high even though puppies with acrodermatitis rarely reach two years of age.

Other inherited skin problems are usually not as fatal as acrodermatitis. All inherited diseases must be diagnosed and treated by a veterinary specialist. There are active programmes being undertaken by many veterinary pharmaceutical manufacturers to solve most, if not all, of the common skin problems of dogs.

PARASITE BITES

Many of us are allergic to insect bites. The bites itch, erupt and may even become infected. Dogs have the same reaction to fleas,

> **DID YOU KNOW?**
>
> Feeding your dog properly is very important. An incorrect diet could affect the dog's health, behaviour and nervous system, possibly making a normal dog into an aggressive one.

> **DID YOU KNOW?**
>
> There is a 25% chance of a puppy getting this fatal gene combination from two parents with recessive genes for acrodermatitis:
>
> AA= NORMAL, HEALTHY
> aa= FATAL
> Aa= RECESSIVE, NORMAL APPEARING
>
> If the female parent has an Aa gene and the male parent has an Aa gene, the chances are one in four that the puppy will have the fatal genetic combination aa.

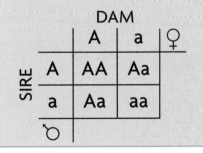

ticks and/or mites. When an insect lands on you, you have the chance to whisk it away with your hand. Unfortunately, when our dog is bitten by a flea, tick or mite, it can only scratch it away or bite it. By the time the dog has been bitten, the parasite has done some of its damage. It may also have laid eggs to cause further problems in the near future. The itching from parasite bites is probably due to the saliva injected into the site when the parasite sucks the dog's blood.

Auto-Immune Skin Conditions

Auto-immune skin conditions are commonly referred to as being allergic to yourself, whilst allergies are usually inflammatory reactions to an outside stimulus. Auto-immune diseases cause serious damage to the tissues that are involved.

The best known auto-immune disease is lupus, which affects people as well as dogs. The symptoms are variable and may affect the kidneys, bones, blood chemistry and skin. It can be fatal to both dogs and humans, though it is not thought to be transmissible. It is usually successfully treated with cortisone, prednisone or similar corticosteroid, but extensive use of these drugs can have harmful side effects.

Parasite Bites

Many of us are allergic to mosquito bites. The bites itch, erupt and may even become infected. Dogs have the same reaction to fleas, ticks and/or mites. When you feel the prick of the mosquito when it bites you, you have a chance to kill it with your hand. Unfortunately, when our dog is bitten by a flea, tick or mite, it can only scratch it away or bite it. By the time the dog has been bitten, the parasite has done some of its damage. It may also have laid eggs to cause further problems in the near future. The itching from parasite bites is probably due to the saliva injected into the site when the parasite sucks the dog's blood.

Airborne Allergies

An interesting allergy is pollen allergy. Humans have hay fever, rose fever and other fevers with which they suffer during the pollinating season. Many dogs suffer the same allergies. When the pollen count is high, your dog might suffer but don't expect them to sneeze and have runny noses like humans. Dogs react to pollen allergies the same way they react to fleas—they scratch and bite themselves.

Dogs, like humans, can be tested for allergens. Discuss the testing with your veterinary dermatologist.

FOOD PROBLEMS

Food Allergies

Dogs are allergic to many foods that are best-sellers and highly recommended by breeders and veterinary surgeons. Changing the brand of food that you buy may not eliminate the problem if the element to which the dog is allergic is contained in the new brand.

Recognising a food allergy is difficult. Humans vomit or have rashes when they eat a food to which they are allergic. Dogs neither vomit nor (usually) develop a rash. They react in the same manner as they do to an airborne or flea allergy: they itch, scratch and bite. Thus making the diagnosis extremely difficult. Whilst pollen allergies and parasite bites are usually seasonal, food allergies are year-round problems.

FOOD INTOLERANCE

Food intolerance is the inability of the dog to completely digest certain foods. Puppies that may have done very well on their mother's milk may not do well on cow's milk. The result of this food intolerance may be loose bowels, passing gas and stomach pains. These are the only obvious symptoms of food intolerance and that makes diagnosis difficult.

TREATING FOOD PROBLEMS

It is possible to handle food allergies and food intolerance yourself. Put your dog on a diet that it has never had. Obviously if it has never eaten this new food it can't have been allergic or intolerant of it. Start with a single ingredient that is not in the dog's diet at the present time. Ingredients like chopped beef or fish are common in dog's diets, so try something more exotic like rabbit, pheasant or even just vegetables. Keep the

dog on this diet (with no additives) for a month. If the symptoms of food allergy or intolerance disappear, chances are your dog has a food allergy.

Don't think that the single ingredient cured the problem. You still must find a suitable diet and ascertain which ingredient in the old diet was objectionable. This is most easily done by adding ingredients to the new diet one at a

DID YOU KNOW?

Your dog's protein needs are change-able. High activity level, stress, climate and other physical factors may require your dog to have more protein in his diet. Check with your veterinary surgeon.

time. Let the dog stay on the modified diet for a month before you add another ingredient. Eventually, you will determine the ingredient that caused the adverse reaction.

An alternative method is to carefully study the ingredients in the diet to which your dog is allergic or intolerable. Identify the main ingredient in this diet and eliminate the main ingredient by buying a different food that does not have that ingredient. Keep experimenting until the symptoms disappear after one month on the new diet.

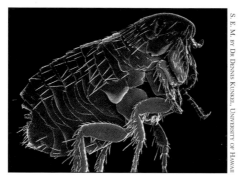

A scanning electron micrograph (S. E. M.) of a dog flea, *Ctenocephalides canis.*

S. E. M. BY DR DENNIS KUNKEL, UNIVERSITY OF HAWAII

EXTERNAL PARASITES

Of all the problems to which dogs are prone, none is more well known and frustrating than fleas. Fleas, which usually refers to fleas, ticks and mites, are relatively simple to cure but difficult to prevent. Parasites that are harboured inside the body are a bit more difficult to cure but they are easier to control.

FLEAS

To control a flea infestation you have to understand its life cycle. Fleas are often thought of as a

summertime problem but centrally heated homes have changed the patterns and fleas can be found at any time of the year. Their effective treatment (destruction) is environmental. Unfortunately, no single flea control medicine (insecticide) is effective in every flea infested area. To understand flea control you must apply suitable treatment to the weak link in the life cycle of the flea.

THE LIFE CYCLE OF A FLEA

Fleas are found in four forms: eggs, larvae, pupae and adults. You really need a low-power microscope or hand lens to

Magnified head of a dog flea, *Ctenocephalides canis.*

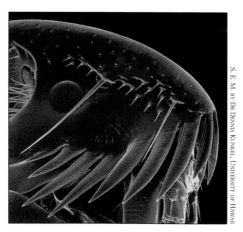

S. E. M. BY DR DENNIS KUNKEL, UNIVERSITY OF HAWAII

DID YOU KNOW?

Fleas have been around for millions of years and have adapted to changing host animals.

They are able to go through a complete life cycle in less than one month or they can extend their lives to almost two years by remaining as pupae or cocoons. They do not need blood or any other food for up to 20 months.

They have been measured as being able to jump 300,000 times and can jump 150 times their length in any direction including straight up. Those are just a few of the reasons they are so successful in infesting a dog!

DID YOU KNOW?

Flea-killers are poisonous. You should not spray these toxic chemicals on areas of the dog's body that he licks, on his genitals or on his face. Flea-killers taken internally are a better answer, but check with your vet in case internal therapy is not advised for your dog.

identify a living flea's eggs, pupae or larva. They spend their whole lives on your Lhasa Apso unless they are forcibly removed by brushing, bathing, scratching or biting.

Several species infest both dog and cats. The dog flea is scientifically known as *Ctenocephalides canis* while the cat flea is *Ctenocephalides felis*. Cat fleas are very common on dogs.

DID YOU KNOW?

Dogs who have been exposed to lawns sprayed with herbicides have double and triple the rate of malignant lymphoma. Town dogs are especially at risk, as they are exposed to tailored yards and gardens. Dogs perspire and absorb through their footpads. Be careful where your dog walks and always avoid any area that appears yellowed from chemical overspray.

Fleas lay eggs while they are in residence on your dog. These eggs do not adhere to the hair of your dog and they fall off almost as soon as they dry (they may be a bit damp when initially laid). These eggs are the reservoir of future flea infestations. If your dog scratches himself and is able to dislodge a few fleas, they simply fall off and await a future chance to attack a dog...or a person. Yes, fleas from dogs bite people. That's why it is so important to control fleas both on the dog and in the dog's entire environment. You must, therefore, treat the dog and the environment simultaneously.

DID YOU KNOW?

There are many parasiticides which can be used around your home and garden to control fleas.

Natural pyrethrins can be used inside the house.

Allethrin, bioallethrin, permethrin and resmethrin can also be used inside the house but permethrin has been used successfully outdoors, too.

Carbaryl can be used indoors and outdoors.

Propoxur can be used indoors.

Chlorpyrifos, diazinon and malathion can be used indoors or outdoors and it has an extended residual activity.

133

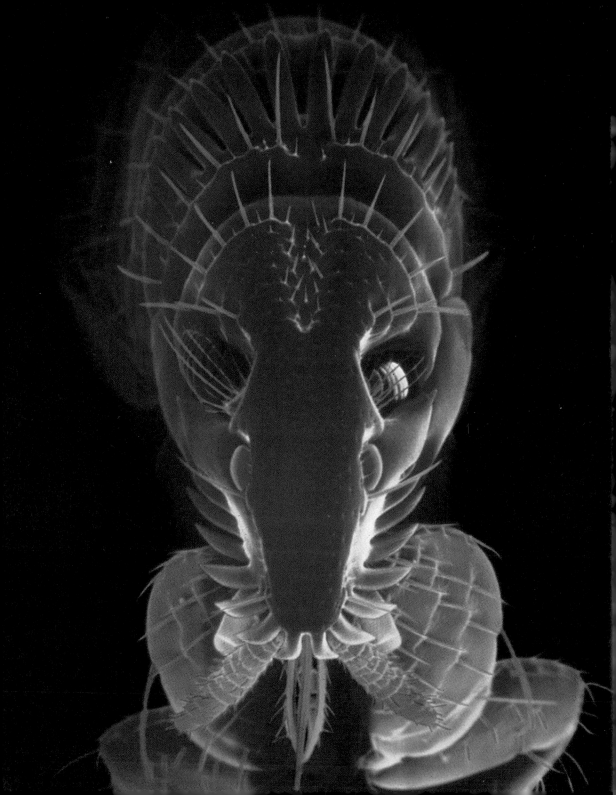

DE-FLEAING THE HOME

Cleanliness is the simple rule. If you have a cat living with your dog, the matter is more complicated since most dog fleas are actually cat fleas. Cats climb onto many areas that are never accessible to dogs (like window sills, table tops, etc.), so you will have to clean all of these areas, too. The hard floor surfaces (tiles, wood, stone and linoleum) must be mopped several times a day. Drops of food onto the floor are actually food for flea larvae! All rugs and furniture must be vacuumed several times a day. Don't forget cupboards, under furniture, cushions. A study has reported that a vacuum cleaner with a beater bar can remove only

A male dog flea, *Ctenocephalides canis*.

PHOTO BY JEAN CLAUDE REVY/PHOTOTAKE.

DID YOU KNOW?

Never mix flea control products without first consulting your veterinary surgeon. Some products can become toxic when combined with others and can cause serious or fatal consequences.

20% of the larvae and 50% of the eggs. The vacuum bags should be discarded into a sealed plastic bag or burned. The vacuum machine itself should be cleaned. The outdoor area to which your dog has access must also be treated with an insecticide.

DID YOU KNOW?

Ivermectin is quickly becoming the drug of choice for treating many parasitic skin diseases in dogs.

For some unknown reason, herding dogs like Collies, Old English Sheepdogs and German Shepherds, etc., are extremely sensitive to ivermectin.

Ivermectin injections have killed some dogs. The ivermectin reaction is a toxicosis which causes tremors, loss of power to move their muscles, prolonged dilatation of the pupil of the eye, coma (unconsciousness), or cessation of breathing (death).

The toxicosis usually starts from 4-6 hours after ingestion or as late as 12 hours. The longer it takes to set in, the milder is the reaction.

Ivermectin should only be prescribed and administered by a vet.

Some ivermectin treatments require two doses.

Opposite page: A scanning electron micrograph of a dog or cat flea, *Ctenocephalides*, magnified more than 100x. This has been colourised for effect.

Male cat fleas, *Ctenocephalides felis*, are very commonly found on dogs.

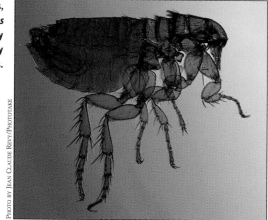

PHOTO BY JEAN CLAUDE REVY/PHOTOTAKE

STERILISING THE ENVIRONMENT
Besides cleaning your home with vacuum cleaners and mops, you have to treat the outdoor range of your dog. This means trimming bushes and spreading insecticide.Be careful not to poison areas in which fishes or other animals reside.

TICKS AND MITES
Though not as common as fleas, ticks and mites are found all over the tropical and temperate world. They don't bite, like fleas; they harpoon. They dig their sharp proboscis (nose) into the dog's skin and drink the blood. Their only food and drink is dog's blood. Dogs can get Lyme disease, Rocky

Your vet will be able to recommend a household insecticidal spray but this must be used with caution, and instructions strictly adhered to.

While there are many drugs available to kill fleas on the dog itself, such as the

Dwight R. Kuhn's magnificent action photo showing a flea jumping from a dog's back.

miracle drug ivermectin, it is best to have the de-fleaing and de-worming supervised by your vet. Ivermectin is effective against many external and internal parasites including heartworms, roundworms, tapeworms, flukes, ticks and mites. It has not been approved for use to control these pests, but veterinary surgeons frequently use it anyway. Ivermectin may not be available in all areas.

PHOTO BY DWIGHT R KUHN

136

The Life Cycle of the Flea

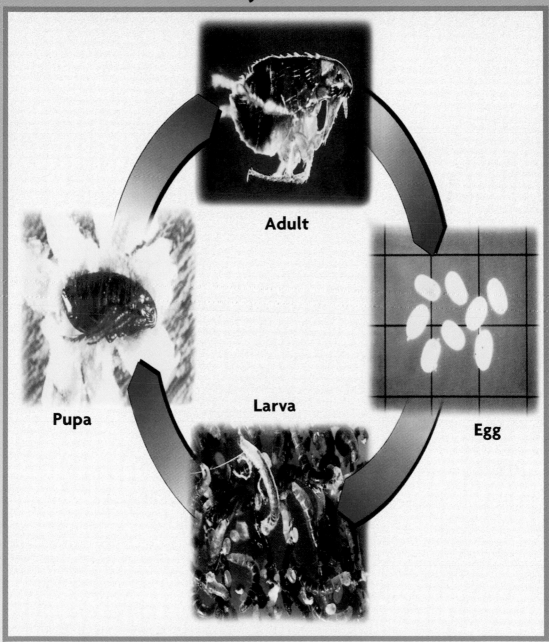

Adult

Pupa

Larva

Egg

The life cycle of the flea was posterised by Fleabusters®. Poster Courtesy of Fleabusters®, R$_x$ for Fleas.

Dog flea eggs magnified.

Mountain spotted fever (normally found in the USA only), paralysis and many other diseases from ticks and mites. They may live where fleas are found and they like to hide in cracks or seams in walls wherever dogs live. They are controlled the same way fleas are controlled.

The dog tick, *Dermacentor variabilis*, may well be the most

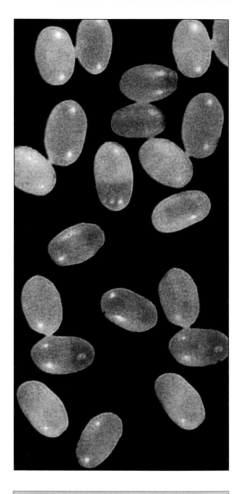

DID YOU KNOW?

There are drugs which prevent fleas from maturing from egg to adult.

The weak link is the maturation from a larva to a pupa.

Methoprene and fenoxycarb mimic the effect of maturation enhancers, thus, in effect, killing the larva before it pupates.

Methoprene is very effective in killing flea eggs while fenoxycarb is better able to stand UV rays from the sun. There is a combination of both drugs which has an effective life of 6 months and destroys 93% of the flea population.

It is important, in order to effectively control fleas, that you use products designed to kill fleas at all stages of growth, Manufacturers make such products, which are specifically designed for this purpose, and specially made to be safe for use in the home and on the dog.

DID YOU KNOW?

Never allow your dog to swim in polluted water or public areas where water quality can be suspect. Even perfectly clear water can harbour parasites, many of which can cause serious to fatal illnesses in canines. Areas inhabited by waterfowl and other wildlife are especially dangerous.

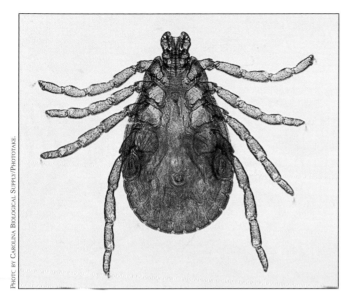

PHOTO BY CAROLINA BIOLOGICAL SUPPLY/PHOTOTAKE.

The non-contagious mites are *Demodex*. The most serious of the mites is the ear mite infestation. Ear mites are usually controlled with ivermectin.

It is essential that your dog be treated for mange as quickly as possible because some forms of mange are transmissible to people.

A brown dog tick, *Rhipicephalus sanguineus*, is an uncommon but annoying tick found on dogs.

common dog tick in many geographical areas, especially those areas where the climate is hot and humid.

Most dog ticks have life expectancies of a week to six months, depending upon climatic conditions. They can neither jump nor fly, but they can crawl slowly and can range up to 5 metres (16 feet) to reach a sleeping or unsuspecting dog.

MANGE

Mites cause a skin irritation called mange. Some are contagious, like *Cheyletiella*, ear mites, scabies and chiggers.

PHOTO BY DWIGHT R KUHN.

Human lice look like dog lice; the two are closely related.

139

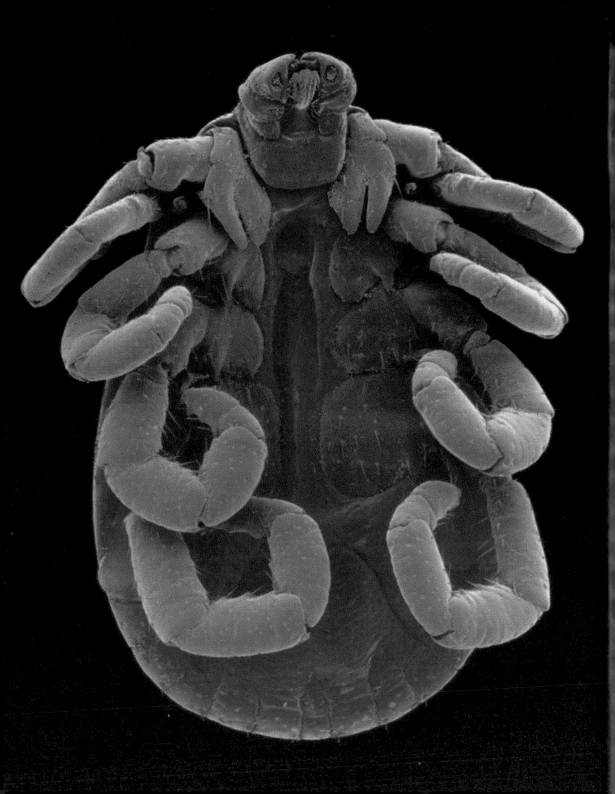

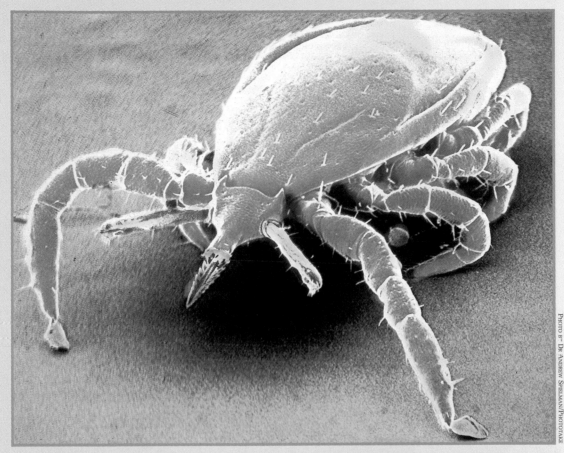

Photo by Dr Andrew Spielman/Phototake

A deer tick, the carrier of Lyme disease.

Opposite page:
The dog tick,
*Dermacentor
variabilis*, is
probably the most
common tick
found on dogs.
Look at the
strength in its
eight legs! No
wonder it's hard to
detach them.

S. E. M. by Dr Dennis Kinzel, University of Hawaii.

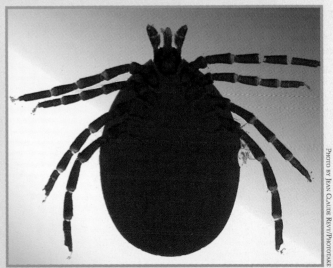

An uncommon
dog tick of the
genus *Ixode*.
Magnified 10x.

Photo by Jean Claude Revy/Phototake

Two views of the mange mite, Psoroptes bovis.

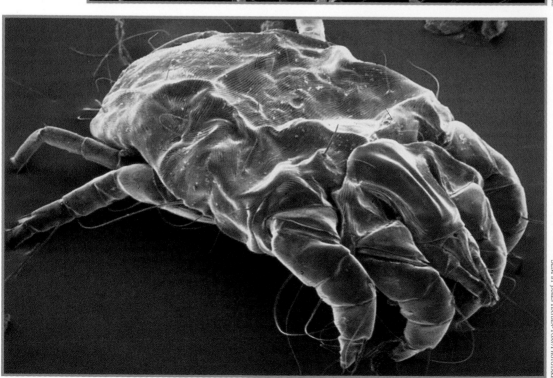

SEM by Dennis Kunkel, University of Hawaii.

INTERNAL PARASITES

Most animals—fishes, birds and mammals, including dogs and humans—have worms and other parasites that live inside their bodies. According to Dr Herbert R Axelrod, the fish pathologist, there are two kinds of parasites: dumb and smart. The smart parasites live in peaceful coopera-tion with their hosts (symbiosis), while the dumb parasites kill their host. Most of the worm infections are relatively easy to control. If they are not controlled they eventually weaken the host dog to the point that other medical problems occur, but they are not dumb parasites.

ROUNDWORMS

The roundworms that infect dogs are scientifically known as *Toxocara canis*. They live in the dog's intestine. The worms shed eggs continually. It has been estimated that a dog produces about 150 grammes of faeces every day. Each gramme of faeces averages 10,000–12,000 eggs of roundworms. There are no known areas in which dogs roam that do not contain roundworm eggs. The greatest danger of roundworms is that they infect

The head of the dog tick, *Dermacentor variabilis.*

DID YOU KNOW?

Ridding your puppy of worms is VERY IMPORTANT because certain worms that puppies carry, such as tapeworms and roundworms, can infect humans.

Breeders initiate a deworming programme at or about four weeks of age. The routine is repeated every two or three weeks until the puppy is three months old. The breeder from whom you obtained your puppy should provide you with the complete details of the deworming programme.

Your veterinary surgeon can prescribe and monitor the programme of deworming for you. The usual programme is treating the puppy every 15 to 20 days until the puppy is positively worm free.

It is not advised that you treat your puppy with drugs that are not recommended professionally.

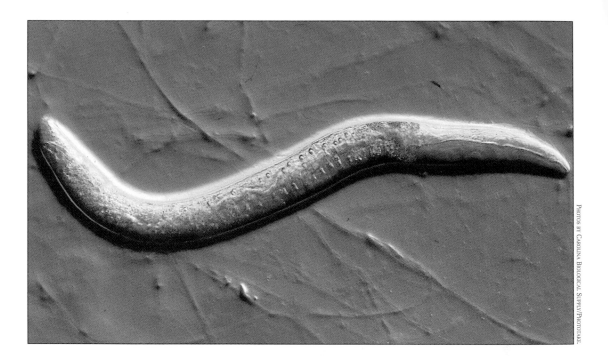

Two views of the roundworm, *Rhabditis*. The roundworm can infect both dogs and humans.

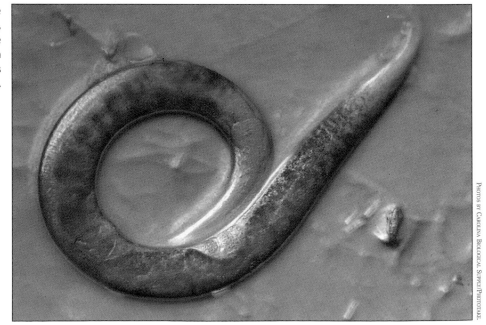

people, too! It is wise to have your dog tested regularly for roundworms.

Pigs also have roundworm infections that can be passed to human and dogs. The typical roundworm parasite is called *Ascaris lumbricoides*.

DID YOU KNOW?

Humans, rats, squirrels, foxes, coyotes, wolves, mixed breeds of dogs and purebred dogs are all susceptible to tapeworm infection. Except in humans, tapeworms are usually not a fatal infection. Infected individuals can harbour a thousand parasitic worms. Tapeworms have two sexes—male and female (many other worms have only one sex—male and female in the same worm). If dogs eat infected rats or mice, they get the tapeworm disease.

One month after attaching to a dog's intestine, the worm starts shedding eggs. These eggs are infective immediately. Infective eggs can live for a few months without a host animal. Roundworms, whipworms and tapeworms are just a few of the other commonly known worms that infect dogs.

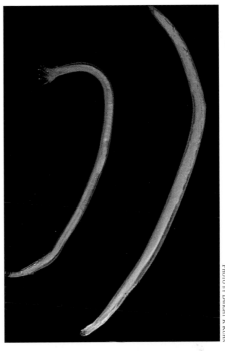

Male and female hookworms, *Ancylostoma caninum*, are uncommonly found in pet or show dogs in Britain. Hookworms may infect other dogs that have exposure to grasslands.

PHOTO BY DWIGHT R KUHN

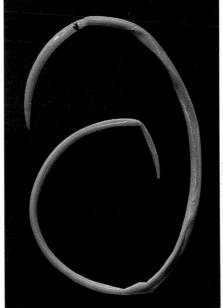

The roundworm *Rhabditis*.

PHOTO BY CAROLINA BIOLOGICAL SUPPLY/PHOTOTAKE

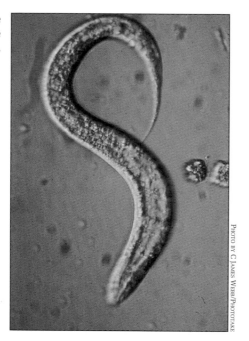

The infective stage of the hookworm larva.

PHOTO BY C JAMES WEBB/PHOTOTAKE

HOOKWORMS

The worm *Ancylostoma caninum* is commonly called the dog hookworm. It is dangerous to humans and cats. It also has teeth by which it attaches itself to the intestines of the dog. It changes the site of its attachment about six times a day and the dog loses blood from each detachment, possibly causing iron-deficiency anaemia. They are easily purged from the dog with many medications, the best of which seems to be ivermectin even though it has not been approved for such use.

In Britain the 'temperate climate' hookworm (*Uncinaria stenocephala*) is rarely found in

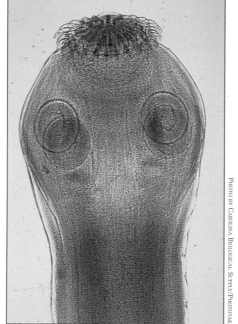

The head and rostellum (the round prominence on the scolex) of a tapeworm, which infects dogs and humans.

PHOTO BY CAROLINA BIOLOGICAL SUPPLY/PHOTOTAKE

DID YOU KNOW?

Average size dogs can pass 1,360,000 roundworm eggs every day.

For example, if there were only 1 million dogs in the world, the world would be saturated with 1,300 metric tonnes of dog faeces. These faeces would contain 15,000,000,000 roundworm eggs.

7 to 31 percent of home gardens and children's play boxes in the U. S. contained roundworm eggs.

Flushing dog's faeces down the toilet is not a safe practice because the usual sewage treatments do not destroy roundworm eggs.

Infected puppies start shedding roundworm eggs at 3 weeks of age. They can be infected by their mother's milk.

pet or show dogs, but can occur in hunting packs, racing Greyhounds and sheepdogs because the worms can be prevalent wherever dogs are exercised regularly on grassland.

TAPEWORMS
There are many species of tapeworms. They are carried by fleas! The dog eats the flea and starts the tapeworm cycle. Humans can also be infected with tapeworms, so don't eat fleas! Fleas are so small that your dog could pass them onto your hands, your plate or your food and thus make it possible for you to ingest a flea which is carrying tapeworm eggs.

While tapeworm infection is not life threatening in dogs (smart parasite!), it can be the cause of a very serious liver disease for humans. About 50 percent of the humans infected with *Echinococcus multilocularis*, a type of tapeworm that causes alveolar hydatis, perish.

HEARTWORMS
Heartworms are thin, extended worms up to 30 cms (12 ins) long which live in a dog's heart and the major blood vessels surrounding it. Dogs may have up to 200 of these worms. The symptoms may be loss of energy, loss of appetite, coughing, the development of a pot belly and anaemia.

Heartworms are transmitted

DID YOU KNOW?

You are your dog's caretaker and his dentist. Vets warn that plaque and tartar buildup on the teeth will damage the gums and allow bacteria to enter the dog's bloodstream, causing serious damage to the animal's vital organs. Studies show that over 50 percent of dogs have some form of gum disease before age three. Daily or weekly tooth cleaning (with a brush or soft gauze pad wipes) can add years to your dog's life.

by mosquitoes. The mosquito drinks the blood of an infected dog and takes in larvae with the blood. The larvae, called microfilaria, develop within the body of the mosquito and are passed on to the next dog bitten after the larvae mature. It takes two to three weeks for the larvae to develop to the infective stage within the body of the mosquito. Dogs should be treated at about six weeks of age, then every six months.

Blood testing for heartworms is not necessarily indicative of how seriously your dog is infected. This is a dangerous disease. Although heartworm is a problem for dogs in America, Australia, Asia and Central Europe, dogs in the United Kingdom are not affected by heartworm.

When you purchased your Lhasa Apso you will have made it clear to the breeder whether you wanted one just as a loveable companion and pet, or if you hoped to be buying a Lhasa Apso with show prospects. No reputable breeder will have sold you a young puppy saying that it was definitely of show quality for so much can go wrong during the early weeks and months of a puppy's development. If you plan to show, what you will hopefully have acquired is a puppy with 'show potential'.

To the novice, exhibiting a Lhasa Apso in the show ring may look easy but it usually takes a lot of hard work and devotion to do top winning at a show such as the prestigious Crufts, not to mention a little luck too!

The first concept that the canine novice learns when watching a dog show is that each breed first competes against members of its own breed. Once the judge has selected the best member of each breed, provided that the show is judged on a Group system, that chosen dog will compete with other dogs in its group. Finally the best of each group will compete for Best in Show and Reserve Best in Show.

The second concept that you must understand is that the dogs are not actually competing against one another. The judge compares each dog against the breed standard, which is a written description of the ideal specimen of the breed. Whilst some early breed standards were indeed

DID YOU KNOW?

The Kennel Club divides its dogs into seven Groups: Gundogs, Utility, Working, Toy, Terrier, Hounds and Pastoral.*

*The Pastoral Group, established in 1999, includes those sheepdog breeds previously categorised in the Working Group.

based on specific dogs that were famous or popular, many dedicated enthusiasts say that a perfect specimen, described in the

standard, has never been bred. Thus the 'perfect' dog never walked into a show ring, has never been bred and, to the woe of dog breeders around the globe, does not exist. Breeders attempt to get as close to this ideal as possible, with every litter, but theoretically the 'perfect' dog is so elusive that it is impossible. (And if the 'perfect' dog were born, breeders and judges would never agree that it was indeed 'perfect.')

If you are interested in exploring dog shows, your best bet is to join your local breed club. These clubs often host both Championship and Open shows, and sometimes Match meetings and Special Events, all of which

could be of interest, even if you are only an onlooker. Clubs also send out newsletters and some organise training days and seminars in order that people may learn more about their chosen breed. To locate the nearest breed club for you, contact The Kennel Club, the ruling body for the British dog world. The Kennel Club governs not only conformation shows but also working trials, obedience trials, agility trials and field trials. The Kennel Club furnishes the rules and regulations for all these events plus general dog registration and other basic requirements of dog ownership. Its annual show called the Crufts Dogs Show, held in Birmingham, is the largest bench show in England. Every year over 20,000 of the U.K.'s best dogs qualify to participate in this

Winners of the bitch classes at a breed championship show in Australia.

WINNING THE TICKET

Earning a championship at Kennel Club shows is the most difficult in the world. Compared to the United States and Canada where it is relatively not 'challenging,' collecting three green tickets not only requires much time and effort, it can be very expensive! Challenge Certificates, as the tickets are properly known, are the building blocks of champions—good breeding, good handling, good training and good luck!

marvellous show which lasts four days.

The Kennel Club governs many different kinds of shows in Great Britain, Australia, South Africa and beyond. At the most competitive and prestigious of these shows, the Championship Shows, a dog can earn Challenge Certificates, and thereby become a Show Champion or a Champion. A dog must earn three Challenge Certificates under three different judges to earn the prefix of 'Sh Ch' or 'Ch.' Note that some breeds must also qualify in a field trial in order to gain the title of full champion. Challenge Certificates are awarded to a very small percentage of the dogs competing, especially as dogs which are

HOW TO ENTER A DOG SHOW

1. Obtain an entry form and show schedule from the Show Secretary.
2. Select the classes that you want to enter and complete the entry form.
3. Transfer your dog into your name at The Kennel Club. (Be sure that this matter is handled before entering.)
4. Find out how far in advance show entries must be made. Oftentimes it's more than a couple of months.

already Champions compete with others for these coveted CCs. The number of Challenge Certificates awarded in any one year is based upon the total number of dogs in each breed entered for competition. There three types of Championship Shows, an all-breed General Championship show for all Kennel Club recognised, a Group Championship Show, limited to breeds within one of the groups, and a Breed Show, usually confined to a single breed. The Kennel Club determines which breeds at which Championship Shows will have the opportunity to earn Challenge Certificates (or tickets). Serious exhibitors often will opt not to participate if the tickets are withheld at a particular show. This policy makes earning

CLASSES AT DOG SHOWS

There can be as many as 18 classes per sex for your breed. Check the show schedule carefully to make sure that you have entered your dog in the appropriate class. Among the classes offered can be: Beginners; Minor Puppy (ages 6 to 9 months); Puppy (ages 6 to 12 months); Junior (ages 6 to 18 months); Beginners (handler or dog never won first place) as well as the following, each of which is defined in the schedule: Maiden; Novice; Tyro; Debutant; Undergraduate; Graduate; Postgraduate; Minor Limit; Mid Limit; Limit; Open; Veteran; Stud Dog; Brood Bitch; Progeny; Brace and Team.

championships ever more difficult to accomplish.

Open Shows are generally less competitive and are frequently used as 'practice shows' for young dogs. There are hundreds of Open Shows each year that can be invitingly social events and are great first show experiences for the novice. Even if you're considering just watching a show to wet your paws, an Open Show is a great choice.

Whilst Championship and Open Shows are most important for the beginner to understand, there are other types of shows in which the interested dog owner can participate. Training clubs sponsor Matches that can be entered on the day of the show for a nominal fee. In these introductory-level exhibitions, two dogs are pulled out of a hat and 'matched,' the winner of that match goes on to the next round, and eventually only one dog is left undefeated.

Exemption Shows are much more light-hearted affairs with usually only four pedigree classes and several 'fun' classes, all of which can be entered on the day. The proceeds of an Exemption Show must be given to a charity and are sometimes held in conjunction with small agricultural shows. Limited Shows are also available in small number, but entry is restricted to members of the club which hosts the show, although one can usually join the

There is a lot of action as Lhasa Apsos are prepared for their turn in the ring at an outdoor breed show in Australia.

DID YOU KNOW?

Just like with anything else, there is a certain etiquette to the show ring that can only be learned through experience. Showing your dog can be quite intimidating to you as a novice when it seems as if everyone else knows what he's doing. You can familiarise yourself with ring procedure beforehand by taking a class to prepare you and your dog for conformation showing or by talking with an experienced handler. When you are in the ring, listen and pay attention to the judge and follow his/her directions. Remember, even the most skilled handlers had to start somewhere. Keep it up and you too will become a proficient handler before too long!

club when making an entry.

Before you actually step into the ring, you would be well advised to sit back and observe the judge's ring procedure. If it is your first time in the ring, do not be over-anxious and run to the front of the line. It is much better to stand back and study how the exhibitor in front of you is performing. The judge asks each handler to 'stand' the dog, hopefully showing the dog off to his best advantage. The judge will observe the dog from a distance and from different angles, approach the dog, check his teeth, overall structure, alertness and

DID YOU KNOW?

There are 329 breeds recognised by the FCI, and each breed is considered to be 'owned' by a specific country. Each breed standard is a cooperative effort between the breed's country and the FCI's Standards and Scientific Commissions. Judges use these official breed standards at shows held in FCI member countries. One of the functions of the FCI is to update and translate the breed standards into French, English, Spanish and German.

muscle tone, as well as consider how well the dog 'conforms' to the standard. Most importantly, the judge will have the exhibitor move the dog around the ring in some pattern that he or she should specify (another advantage to not going first, but always listen since some judges change their directions, and the judge is always right!) Finally the judge will give the dog one last look before moving on to the next exhibitor.

If you are not in the top three at your first show, do not be discouraged. Be patient and consistent and you may eventually find yourself in the winning lineup. Remember that the winners were once in your shoes and have devoted many hours and much money to earn the

DID YOU KNOW?

FCI-recognised breeds are divided into ten groups:
Group 1: Sheepdogs and Cattledogs (except Swiss Cattledogs)
Group 2: Pinschers and Schnauzers, Molossians, Swiss Mountain Dogs and Swiss Cattledogs
Group 3: Terriers
Group 4: Dachshunds
Group 5: Spitz- and primitive-type dogs
Group 6: Scenthounds and related breeds
Group 7: Pointing dogs
Group 8: Retrievers, Flushing dogs and Water dogs
Group 9: Companion and Toy dogs
Group 10: Sighthounds

Best in Show winner at Tibethund, held in Sweden, judged by the author.

placement. If you find that your dog is losing every time and never getting a nod, it may be time to consider a different dog sport or just enjoy your Lhasa Apso as a pet.

WORKING TRIALS

Working trials can be entered by any well-trained dog of any breed, not just Gundogs or Working dogs. Many dogs that earn the Kennel Club Good Citizen Dog award choose to participate in a working trial. There are five stakes at both open and championship levels: Companion Dog (CD), Utility Dog (UD), Working Dog (WD), Tracking Dog (TD), and Patrol Dog (PD). As in conformation shows, dogs compete against a standard and if

DID YOU KNOW?

You can get information about dog shows from kennel clubs and breed clubs:

Fédération Cynologique Internationale
14, rue Leopold II, B-6530 Thuin, Belgium
www.fci.be

The Kennel Club
1-5 Clarges St., Piccadilly, London W1Y 8AB, UK
www.the-kennel-club.org.uk

American Kennel Club
5580 Centerview Dr., Raleigh, NC 27606-3390, USA
www.akc.org

Canadian Kennel Club
89 Skyway Ave., Suite 100, Etobicoke, Ontario M9W 6R4 Canada
www.ckc.ca

the dog reaches the qualifying mark, it obtains a certificate. Divided into groups, each exercise must be achieved 70 percent in order to qualify. If the dog achieves 80 percent in the open level, it receives a Certificate of Merit (COM), in the championship level, it receives a Qualifying Certificate. At the CD stake, dogs must participate in four groups, Control, Stay, Agility and Search (Retrieve and Nosework). At the next three levels, UD, WD and TD, there are only three groups: Control, Agility and Nosework.

Agility consists of three jumps: a vertical scale up a wall of planks; a clear jump over a basic hurdle with a removable top bar; and a long jump across angled planks.

To earn the UD, WD and TD, dogs must track approximately one-half mile for articles laid from one-half hour to three hours ago. Tracks consist of turns and legs, and fresh ground is used for each participant.

The fifth stake, PD, involves teaching manwork, which is not recommended for every breed.

AGILITY TRIALS
Agility trials began in the United Kingdom in 1977 and have since spread around the world, especially to the United States, where it enjoys strong popularity. The handler directs his dog over an obstacle course that includes jumps (such as those used in the working trials), as well as tyres, the dog walk, weave poles, pipe tunnels, collapsed tunnels, etc. The Kennel Club requires that dogs not be trained for agility until they are 12 months old. This dog sport intends to be great fun for dog and owner and interested owners should join a training club that has obstacles and experienced agility handlers who can introduce you and your dog to the 'ropes' (and tyres, tunnels and so on).

FÉDÉRATION CYNOLOGIQUE INTERNATIONALE
Established in 1911, the Fédération Cynologique Internationale represents the 'world kennel club.' This international body brings uniformity to the breeding, judging and showing of purebred dogs. Although the FCI originally included only four European nations: France, Holland, Austria and Belgium (which remains its

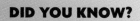

DID YOU KNOW?

The overall structure of the FCI is divided into several bodies:
- General Assembly
- Executive Committee and General Committee
- Compulsory Commissions (Standards, Scientific and Legal)
- Non-compulsory Commissions

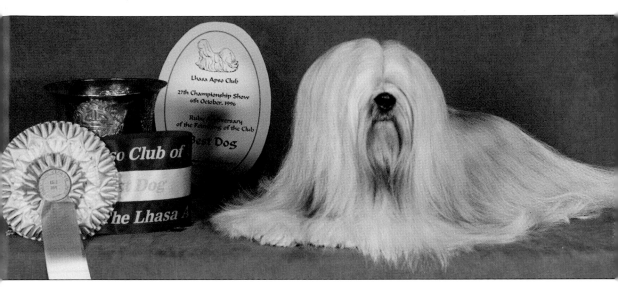

headquarters), the organisation today embraces nations on six continents and recognises well over 300 breeds of purebred dog. There are three titles attainable through the FCI: the International Champion, which is the most prestigious; the International Beauty Champion, which is based on aptitude certificates in different countries; and the International Trial Champion, which is based on achievement in obedience trials in different countries. Quarantine laws in England and Australia prohibit most of their exhibitors from entering FCI shows. The rest of the Continent does participate in these impressive canine spectacles, the largest of which is the World Dog Show, hosted in a different country each year. FCI sponsors both national and international shows The hosting country determines the judging system and breed standards are always based on the breed's country of origin.

This is what it is all about. A magnificent award-winning dog brings a great deal of personal satisfaction and pride to the show dog owner.

DID YOU KNOW?

The FCI *does not* issue pedigrees. The FCI members and contract partners are responsible for issuing pedigrees and training judges in their own countries. The FCI does maintain a list of judges and makes sure that they are recognised throughout the FCI member countries.

The FCI also *does not* act as a breeder referral; breeder information is available from FCI-recognised national canine societies in each of the FCI's member countries.

INDEX
Page numbers in **boldface** indicate illustrations.

𝕸𝖞 𝕷𝖍𝖆𝖘𝖆 𝕬𝖕𝖘𝖔

Dog's Name ___Alfie___

Date ___July 2011___ Photographer ___Tricia___